HIDDEN
SURREY

Christopher Howkins

D0767672

HIDDEN SURREY

Christopher Howkins

with illustrations
by the author

COUNTRYSIDE BOOKS
NEWBURY, BERKSHIRE

COUNTRYSIDE BOOKS
3 Catherine Road
Newbury, Berkshire

ISBN 0 905392 94 9

Cover illustration of The Bourne
taken by the author

Typeset by Acorn Bookwork, Salisbury, Wiltshire
Produced through MRM Associates Ltd., Reading
Printed in England by J.W. Arrowsmith Ltd., Bristol

Introduction

➤ Not another guide book to Surrey I thought, but the voice on the phone went on to ask for one that drew attention to subjects that were not the usual guide book material and thus remained 'hidden'. Now that sounded much more worthwhile. It soon proved difficult in a County so densely populated and so well documented, to find suitable material for some places. For these attention has been drawn to particular aspects that might otherwise be overlooked. Thus at Stoke D'Abernon church the famous brasses have been ignored and attention drawn instead to the chest which is of national importance. At Compton, attention is drawn to White Hart Cottage for being a local rarity, rather than dwell upon the church, which although a national treasure, is otherwise well documented. The best place to hide something is of course right under our noses. Everyday Surrey people overlook interesting items as they go about their day, simply because they've been seen so often they're no longer given consideration. It's the interest of the subjects that remains 'hidden' rather than that they themselves are concealed. Thus, where known, some indication is given of the subject's value, locally and nationally, in terms of age, quality, rarity etc.

Surrey is not a County to discover remote hamlets down lonely country lanes but, having said that, the movement of people in and out of Surrey is considerable. So for many newcomers there will indeed be new places to explore down the lanes. Similarly, the motorways now have provided easy access for a whole new range of explorers.

The Final Selection

Everywhere in Surrey was visited to find the material and to confirm that subjects recorded earlier were still there. It's taken eleven months, over sixty field trips and over two thousand miles. I thought I knew Surrey quite well. Now I know I didn't!

The material is being presented in two volumes, one for the larger places and this one for the smaller. It would have been convenient to have divided the material simply into towns and villages but that doesn't work in Surrey. Many villages are now being engulfed by the expansion of nearby towns. Those developed areas will appear in the second volume.

In selecting material for the individual entries first consideration was given to things which could be seen. I aimed to find two and if one was in a church then I tried to ensure that the second was not. Even that wasn't as simple as it sounds. Thursley is worth a visit for simply being a beautiful rural village but it's not very interesting to write about unless one dwells at length on the church. Conversely, Albury is easy to drive through without hesitation and yet a whole book could be written about it. Certainly there is more of interest in most places than this present volume reveals; this is just a prompter to further exploration.

With this in mind a few places have been given an extended entry. Englefield Green, for example, is used to provide a deeper insight into Victorian street housing while Laleham and Shepperton have been extended to reveal more of the interest in their part of the Thames Valley that has only comparatively recently become part of Surrey as the Borough of Spelthorne.

The Omissions

Obviously the omissions say more about my ignorance than anything else. Nevertheless some things have been deliberately omitted. They are the movable objects, or more pertinently, the re-movable objects. Many beautiful, peculiar and intriguing items have been ruthlessly edited out for their own safety while theft is so rife. If publicised, they disappear like magic with a 'let's get it before anyone else does' response. This is not a handbook for thieves and villagers who requested items be omitted will find I've honoured my promise.

Then at the last minute, in response to a general plea from the police, the manuscript was edited again to remove references to period piece items such as Victorian door furniture, garden gates etc. for which high prices are paid by those refurbishing old properties.

Sadly, as far as this book is concerned, the romanesque jewellery, the renaissance paintings, the classical garden sculpture, the fire assurance plates and much Victoriana will have to remain hidden. There's a wealth of such interest in Surrey but that's not to be taken literally; it's not to be taken at all.

Consequently the book is much concerned with the buildings and village design they create.

Village Design

It's easy to look for particular items of interest. It's much more difficult to stop and look at a place as a whole – in many instances the product of unsympathetic development. If the efforts to reduce the Green Belt restrictions ever succeed then Surrey will change dramatically. Already the farms north of the downs are rapidly disappearing as they are being sold off in small lots; too small for farming. So it's horse paddocks today but what about tomorrow?

Fortunately the best village centres have been designated Conservation Areas by the County Council but vigilance is still essential if Surrey is to have the best – and why shouldn't it have the best? Inevitably there must be changes. The County cannot be 'fossilised' but stress should always be laid upon quality. It certainly hasn't been at Byfleet nor Ashtead but then few modern developments in rural Surrey have been worth a comment. Fortunately, one has now enriched Byfleet. Energetic opposition to change has resulted in some shabby compromises where the development might have been far superior had less energy been expended upon opposition and more upon quality.

The Buildings – Churches

Visiting ancient churches is very popular but some people feel uncomfortable about it. Hopefully, one or two of my entries will encourage these people to overcome their reserve, accept that everyone is welcome, and discover the rich heritage preserved there.

Surrey churches get scant mention in the national books because architecturally they cannot compete with those of East Anglia or the West Country. Nevertheless the County has examples of practically everything you could ask for including a lead font and two wooden fonts, but not an original rood loft. It is to these items of interest, often barely mentioned even in the church guide book, that I've drawn attention.

Additionally, nineteenth century churches are included as they have had the least and often the worst press of all. They represent their own age and community just as much as a medieval one does and are therefore just as interesting. For simple effective interiors try Forest Green and Buckland. For enriched interiors try Holmbury St. Mary and Hascombe. For individuality try Englefield Green and Grafham. There are some horrors of course just as the dirtiest, most unloved one visited was medieval.

Buildings – Domestic

Singling out individual private homes risks invading privacy so comment is usually reserved for groups, such as at Betchworth and Ockley or else fruitful districts such as the farmhouses outside Brockham.

Timber framed houses abound. Hundreds survive, illustrating all the features found in architectural guide books and as there are some cheap pocket books nowadays I haven't gone into detail. To see inside one is rather different but the Crown Inn and Lythe Hill Hotel at Chiddingfold provide two public places. Detellins at Limpsfield is regularly open to the public and the Monastery guest house at Lingfield is now the public library. For a simple cottage,

Oakhurst at Hambledon can be viewed by arrangement. Traditional farm buildings are noticeably falling into decay and need to be savoured quickly; better still, save them altogether. Access for those interested in the timbering is primarily by private arrangement with the owner but a barn at Farley Green has been turned into the village church and the tithe barn from Abinger has been rebuilt as the banqueting hall at Burford Bridge Hotel. Of the other buildings, I've tried to avoid those of purely local interest and chosen ones which fit into broader patterns such as village halls, schools and almshouses.

Wasting time – Church keys

About a third of the churches visited were found to be locked and only Burstow and Ockley had the courtesy to provide directions to the key. It's understandable that churches need locking but not that the location of the key should be such a carefully guarded parish secret. Allow plenty of time to locate it. At Headley there was a printed poster telling anyone where to get the key in case of fire, or at least it would have done if the person who had taken the trouble to pin up the poster had also taken the trouble to fill in the space provided!

Guidance for Disabled People

Accessibility was another criterion when selecting material. The limitations of disability are so varied and people's success at overcoming them so amazing that it was difficult to decide what was inaccessible. Subjects reached by footpath, with mud etc, are noted in the text.

People with restricted mobility but who can nevertheless walk short distances and negotiate steps will probably be able to reach everything in this book. The steps at Titsey church are enormous. Holmbury St. Mary church is up a steep hillside and has a flight of steps too. Oakwood has steepness, mud and gates!

9

People with self-propelled wheelchairs will find the usual problems with kerbs and most of the churches have steps; ramps are a rarity. If you can withstand bumping over steps and have a strong companion who won't be defeated by them then you too will reach practically everything in the book. I wouldn't recommend the three churches noted above.

Wheelchairs that are not self-propelled will certainly come up against obstacles and a scout will be needed. A lot of the material in the book can be spotted without leaving the car.

A Final Smile

Temporary notices around the County are delightful. There was a field jam-packed with cows and a giant hoarding saying 'Pick Your Own'.

Then there was, 'You are requested not to make yourself comfortable in the graveyard" and 'Buses's Only'. For something longer I enjoyed 'This toilet is not open because it is closed due to there being much of the overflowing'.

Thank You

Sincere thanks are due to the dozens of people who have helped with this book – villagers, librarians, local historians and museum curators. Then there has been a gallant band of friends and their children who came on the field trips as map readers and very useful extra pairs of eyes. Thanks are also due to the publishers for the opportunity to embark upon this adventure and all their encouragement not to give up! Keeping on schedule and coping with the masses of material was only possible with the efforts of Chris Wheeler and Sue Harvey. Thank you everybody.

Christopher Howkins

Abinger

➤ The way up to Abinger is long and steep, up lanes cut deep into the hills, upheld with tree roots and enclosed with boughs. It's always a surprise to burst out of the top into a great airy space of wide greens where autumn leaves race and defiant drinkers linger outside the pub.

It's full of surprises. It has the oldest preserved home in Britain; a mesolithic pit dwelling. It has the mound from a Norman wooden castle. It has a Norman church or at least the proportions suggest that. However, it doesn't look quite authentic and inside we read that a flying bomb in 1944 and a lightning strike in 1964 have necessitated much rebuilding. The architect, Frederick Etchells, went to great pains to reconstruct rather than rebuild. It was worth it. The idea of a long narrow nave was retained. The Gothic windows were not. Instead a Norman style fenestration scheme was adopted, to good effect. The walls are softly coloured, not glaring white. The floor is simply flagged. Nothing is overdone. The restraint has not only retained the village church character but even captured something of the 'atmosphere' of a country church.

The very simple chancel enhances the modern east window. It is by one of our foremost stained glass artists, Laurence Lee. For him, good glass should follow the 'straightforward commonsense methods' of the 14th–15th centuries by using 'one's personal images' but they must be 'the authentic language of our times – not just fashionable'. This one catches the eye but does not fight for attention, as it gives out St. Paul's message of life through death, the message of the Cross, and the testimony of this church. The quality must owe a lot to the artist being personally involved in every stage of production of his work, from scale design to finished window.

From his favourite period are three other items of rare interest in Surrey. They are 15th century alabaster panels from the English centre for such things near Nottingham. Between them they show a wide variety of approach from the simple severed head of John the Baptist by the font to the intricate Crucifixion scene in the porch. The latter has so much in so small a tablet yet it is still so clear and effective. It is a masterpiece of design and so skilfully undercut. (There's another at West Horsley, 14th century, weathered).

Before leaving (and there's more to see) notice the head-stone by the lychgate. It makes an interesting comparison with the entry for Newdigate:

> Of sickness sore long time I bore
> I wore my strength away
> Till God was pleased to give me ease
> To take my pains away.
>
> From weakness pain and long disease
> Death set me free when God did please
> I hope this change is for the best
> to live with Christ and be at rest.

Also in the churchyard is a white and shapely war memorial which I'm told is the work of Sir Edwin Lutyens, Surrey's most famous architect. It is very different from his Cenotaph in Whitehall and worth a look at what was then a more modern treatment of a traditional design.

Abinger Hammer

> 'There is no workman that can
> bothe worken wel and hastilie.
> This must be donne at leisure
> parfaitlie.'

So reads an inscribed stone set in the wall at the foot of the slope up to the village school. It is a quotation from Chaucer in the spelling of the Middle English of his day. Opposite is another inscription and this one is in Latin and poor Latin at that I'm told. This makes it more difficult to translate. Literally it probably says 'The greatest part of human wisdom is wanting to not know certain things' or more freely, 'not wanting to know everything'. If this is taken as implying being able to discern 'what is or isn't worth knowing', then it may be too far from the original's intent. With regard to an equivalent English impression we'd probably have to accept 'Knowledge gets in the way of wisdom'. Both inscriptions are a rather surprising choice for a village school but then the school has a surprising tale to tell too.

Like so many others up and down the country it was doomed to closure with recent rounds of educational expenditure cuts. Abinger Hammer, like many others, valued its village school and fought for its retention but unlike many others it had a master card to play. The Local Education Authority didn't actually own the buildings, so all was not lost. It still functions today, administered through the Abinger Hammer Village School Trust.

On the other side of the main road the fresh waters of the river Tillingbourne have been utilised by a watercress farm. It's long been there and taken for granted by Surrey folk, but it may well intrigue outsiders, for there are only forty-five growers registered with the N.F.U.'s Watercress Association. Between them they produce about 5,000 tonnes, worth some £8 million.

As a wild herb, watercress has been valued and gathered since Roman times to ease headaches, rheumatic pain and poor skin. It is rich in vitamins A and E, calcium, iron and dietary fibre. The first modern-type watercress beds were started in 1808 by William Bradbury at Springhead, Kent. So keen were the vendors that London should receive it fresh for breakfast that their street cries were the first to be heard each day. Today you can buy it fresh on site at Abinger Hammer.

Abinger Hammer is an attractive village with large greens bordering the River Tillingbourne. It is strung along the main A25 Guildford to Dorking road, with little car parking space – so choose a quiet time for your exploration.

Albury

➤ Only the high ornate Tudor-style chimneys over the houses in the village street give any indication that maybe here is a tale to tell. It begins at the eastern end where there is access to the Saxon church by the great house in the park.

Around the church was once a village but when fashion changed to the Lord of the Manor living in isolation in his big house in a private park the villagers were persuaded to move by harassment. Thus the present village was founded and the original swept away. Later, in 1819, the banker Henry Drummond bought the park and for forty years made his presence felt.

He built a new church in the new village. It is a copy of one in Thaon in Normandy, except that by mistake it was built of red brick instead of stone. The former manorial chapel in the old church he had refurbished as a mortuary chapel for himself and his family and that is quite a gem of nineteenth century church art. The architect behind it was Pugin, the man who put all the detailing inside and over the outside of the Houses of Parliament. He was having an eventful and emotional life anyway without getting caught up in the village politics stirred by Drummond. His next project was Drummond's park house, by then much altered since its Tudor days and it is not Pugin at his best. It does however have the distinction of sixty-three chimneys, all different and all researched from genuine Tudor originals. Pugin married for a third time, had a mental breakdown and finally died in 1851 ending his works at Albury.

His chimneys over the houses in the street are his most noticeable memorial here. There is no indication that the agricultural poor of Albury suffered so harshly during 'The Hungry Forties' and that in 1830 it was the scene of one of the 'Swing Riots' when the corn mill was deliberately set on fire and the miller shot at. (They missed.) It was the worst time ever for Britain's poor, causing a religious revival with the fervent preaching of the Second Advent of Christ. Henry Drummond became deeply involved with this, turned

16

Albury into an annual conference centre, helped found the Catholic Apostolic Church, was called as an Apostle and spent £15,000 building its first church. That building, in Perpendicular style, still stands near his park gates.

Details of all these activities are for sale in a series of booklets from the Saxon church in the park. Access is from the gateway on the bend in the road at the eastern end of the village by the Catholic Apostolic Church.

Alfold

◄ If you really want something hidden, then try discerning which parts of the church screen are medieval and which parts are closely matching Victorian. In good light the old is often slightly darker and in poor light often feels very slightly warmer.

You'll find a cockerel on one of the beams in the church. It's a former weather vane and a rare chance to see one so closely. I was told it was seventeenth century which is, however, unlikely as vanes were usually a squarish banner at that time. Stylistically there's not much to go by for any date.

Alfold is still very small and remote. The main road has encouraged little development and neither did the Wey Arun Junction Canal when it was operating to the west of the village. Its history is wrapped up with the great Wealden forest and there's fine craftsmanship in wood to prove it. Alfold House, for example, catches the eye by the road and shows how unhelpful some guide books can be when they oversimplify. Some say closely spaced timbering differs in period from the widely spaced. Well here you will find both and the experts say clues in the roof show they followed each other very closely in date.

Further impressive beams can be seen in church supporting the belfry. Although this idea has been used several times in Surrey they are all worth a close look to see exactly how they were constructed. They are all designed to solve the same problem but the solutions all differ. There are two main categories; free standing like Thursley's or bonded into the walls for additional support like Byfleet's. Here at Alfold the crownpost roof of the nave is also worth a close look.

Ash

The fun thing about Ash is to look at a map and note how the different planning authorities have worked. Hampshire has permitted Aldershot to sprawl right up to the county boundary and Surrey has obviously been intent on allowing it no further. To the north, development has been permitted on the former heathlands but to the south of Ash Street the better soils have been kept as farmland with only small hamlets.

Ash Street is long but not without interest. Crooke's Cottages are noticeable more for the contrast with their neighbours than for any inherent quality of their own. Hartshorn, next to the church, is also eye-catching for its brick-filled half-timbering, bulging and buttressed. It is labelled c. 1350 but that's surely the age of the habitation site for what we see looks to be seventeenth century.

Together with Chobham, the church shares the distinction of having a wooden font. Only two others seem to have survived in the whole country for wood was officially outlawed for this purpose as being unworthy.

On the other side of the road, harmonising most unexpectedly with the domestic housing, is the Roman Catholic church. It is a small cruciform building without tower, spire or bell turret, looking very different from the stereotyped image of a Catholic church.

Further down the hill, at last a Surrey County Council school that actually contributes something to the townscape of its location. South Ash School lies high on the bank where the road bends sharply up the hill past the churches. Its modern horizontal emphasis is well suited to its site, enhanced by the retention of the grassy bank in front, when viewed from further down the road. It is a subtle focal point just where one is needed.

Ashtead

◣ Zipped into the main road, the village street curls round the contours and dips attractively in the middle yet architecturally it is disappointing. The Victorians, who worked so hard at the picturesque in Surrey missed this street simply because it wasn't there as such because their main road to Epsom ran behind the church. The turn of the century brought wider buildings with broader gables that are less pleasing. There are some fragments worth a glance but nothing has been done to enhance them or create harmony and the current works are just as insensitive.

At the London end a large nondescript house (apart from the leaf motif texturing the walls) proves to be the almshouses. 'This Hospital was Erected and an annual provision made for the better support and maintenance of six poor widows of this Parish for ever'. That was in 1736 but it had to be 'reinstated' in 1873. It was originally 'By the appointment of ye rt. Hon'ble ye Lady Diana Fielding relict of the Hon'ble Thomas Howard her first Husband and afterwards of the Hon'ble William Fielding'.

You can see her portrait, in marble, on her monument in the church. It is simple but not austere, dignified but not pretentious; a very fine piece of workmanship indeed. She looks down the church renewed in 1862 but invested with that elusive village church 'atmosphere'.

The timber roofs contain a lot of fussy work over the coving and along the wallplates but the beamwork is terrific – all the usual medieval motifs but used with a design and a gusto that are pure nineteenth century.

The church has quite a lot of interest (brasses, glass, font etc.) and the churchyard was well planted with conifers and evergreens which now form a good mature collection.

If you wander around the lanes in this higher part of the village you'll find the best of the interest but nothing very exciting. The Rectory catches the eye with its three bays and shell porch but there are only two dormers and the fenestration is not regular on the bays either. Well House next door does indeed retain its well but it is unexpectedly on top of a bank. In Rectory Lane there is Wisteria Cottage (No.26) of brick but with some half timbering. A little further down is Apple Bough with quite robust half-timbering and white plaster work. Then there is Fowler's Cottage marking the end of that period of building – the timbers are thin, the chimneys have been moved to the ends.

For a complete contrast try the lower part of the village, down Woodfield Lane to the pond and the greens. They've lost their rural qualities and it is the modern housing and shops that are the more noticeable.

Ash Vale

Along the Basingstoke Canal is the more interesting part especially as the waterway never became as derelict as some stretches when the canal went out of use. Boats could still be hired from the boathouse and so it was to the former barge yard here that the Surrey and Hampshire Canal Society came when they embarked upon the mammoth task of restoring the canal.

It nearly had development built over it but in 1969 a petition of 10,000 signatures was handed to representatives from both County Councils requesting their support to save the canal. That was a day that would prove to be vital and now restoration has reached the final stages.

That meeting took place at nearby Ash Lock in the June. By the end of July, Ash Vale barge yard had sheltered the successful building of the first pair of lock gates. Restoration was under way. In June, 1972 there was another celebration at the barge yard when the volunteers had completed a second pair. There have been many great days in this story, a story that proves to be unexpectedly interesting. Ash Lock, filled with boats again in June 1984 evidently gave the greatest satisfaction, but hopefully a greater day will be the opening of the last section so that the route will once again run clear to the Wey Navigation at New Haw and thence to the Thames and the rest of the canal network, or to London and the open seas.

Bagshot

A great banner in red and gold bearing the royal insignia spreads across the north chancel wall of the parish church. It belonged to Field Marshal HRII Arthur, Duke of Connaught and Strathcairn, K.G. He died at Bagshot Park in 1942. On the wall below is his memorial tablet erected by his daughter, Princess Patricia of Connaught. The front pews where he sat are still carpeted in royal blue which can be found again in some pews of the north aisle where lesser members of the royal household sat. The Comptroller of the household for eighteen years is commemorated with two great candlesticks standing in the sanctuary. Lighting all this and more is the fine west window, a memorial to the great matriarch of the family, Queen Victoria. The east window is also a royal donation.

On the back of the vestry door is an inscription recording its use by the Duke for access to Bagshot Park. There, in the early nineteenth century lived the Duchess of Gloucester who employed as garden foreman one John Standish. By 1840 he had set up his own nursery business at Bagshot and was raising his own fuchsias and calceolarias. That was notable enough but he was one of our foremost gardeners, in touch with Robert Fortune, and was rapidly propagating stocks of the new plants introduced from Japan by Fortune. Within ten years he was promoting the new rhododendrons, both from America and Sikkim. He also appointed a garden landscape consultant. So here we have one of the pioneers of the present north west Surrey scene; the large house with landscaped gardens, stately with trees and underplanted with rhododendrons.

Banstead

➤ Banstead – the bean stead or farm – stands high on the downs and has been a place noted since Saxon times. The manor, which stood beside the church, was held by Hubert de Burgh, the supporter of King John, Justiciar of England from 1215 and after the death of the Regent in 1219 became the most powerful man in the land. He fell from that power in 1232 and died here in 1243 but his name lives on in local places like Burgh Wood and Burgh Heath.

Judging from the church architecture, Banstead continued to be of importance, for it has a good Gothic interior, a little more richly done than many in Surrey. There is also a range of memorials which for their own varying reasons are more interesting than usual.

Over the centuries Banstead has also attracted quite a number of visitors who have left us written descriptions of their travels, right up to H. G. Wells in our own time. From them we learn that this was famous sheep and mutton country and also renowned for its herbs. The last is recorded by Mint Road opposite Banstead Place.

This impression of an old downland village will be completely shattered when you get here. It has been ripped open into a long wide straight street bordered with architecture from the worst phase of this century. It is bleak, monotonous and impersonal, drawn into suburbia by the grasp of Croydon.

Betchworth

➤ It's the great chalk pit that is so noticeable nowadays and which has supported a very thriving industry for generations with its own narrow gauge railway etc. Little of great interest remains today.

The standard gauge railway was operating through here by 1850 and was cause for celebration in Broome Park, home

of Sir Benjamin Brodie whose lands included the quarries. They produced more than just chalk and so he gave to nearby Brockham all the stone they needed for building their new church in 1846. Much of the stone was unfit for use as it is so soft and even the best is weathering badly.

It was a generous gesture by a local benefactor who was also the royal surgeon to Queen Victoria, George IV and William IV, and of international standing for his work. Sir Benjamin rose to be President of the Royal College of Surgeons, a master of diagnosis and an early exponent of preventive medicine. There is a marble memorial to him in the south nave wall of the church.

The Saxon church has been reduced to a mere fragment by 13th and 19th century remodellings, but is still a fine building. Repairs and amendments were financed in 1451 by the will of Thomas Morsted, with an annuity of 16 pennies. He was another royal doctor, first to Henry IV, then Henry V and finally Henry VI. Thus he and a team of twelve surgeons travelled with the English army of Henry V, suffered terrible rigours and mopped up the mess from the battle of Agincourt. Later, he was appointed Inspector General of all shipping in the Port of London and also served as Sheriff of that city. Locally he was a benefactor of Brockham as well as Betchworth and held the Manor of Wotton too. Here in Betchworth church is a brass memorial inscription to his parents. A third royal doctor, Sir Dyce Duckworth (died 1928) has had his memorial cross stolen.

Outside, the village is such a contrast to neighbouring Brockham but just as memorable in its own way. The buildings are all squidged into the banks and trees down a long lane from the Downs to the river Mole. A great many date from the seventeenth century and make the best collection of that date in Surrey. At the bottom of the street is Betchworth House of which the oldest parts date from 1625. They're one of two good examples of Carolean architecture in the county.

Next comes the river Mole (bridge 1843; with raised pedestrian prae) and a marvellous scattering of old farms through Holmsdale. For a different view of the Vale try going to Dorking by train. It is a beautiful run and while you're waiting, the domesticated railway architecture at Betchworth station is worth noting.

The picturesque little street that you'll find illustrated in so many guides can be found tucked away on the north side of the church and remains much as it has been for generations. It is similar to that at Farleigh.

It includes a derelict barn but for once that has proved valuable as recently it has enabled the archaeologists to excavate parts of the site to help us understand the life that such a barn has led. I'm told it is hoped to restore the barn.

Bisley

➤ Between 1854 and 1890 but chiefly in 1878 many commons were taken over by the War Department and their common rights extinguished. Great tracts of West Surrey are still military training grounds. Other areas have been built on as military camps, such as Bisley, right on the eastern edge. The old medieval church with its ancient woodwork lies down a little lane even further east.

Bisley Camp is the home of the National Rifle Association and had its own branch line (see Brookwood) to service its annual meetings. That closed in 1952 but the platform and station remain. They have been adopted by the Lloyds Bank Rifle Club who have provided sleeping accommodation for twenty-two members in a former British Rail Sleeping Car, now resting on its specially laid length of track.

Blackheath

There is little here but it represents the foundation of some of the later settlements in Surrey. It was evidently created by squatters taking part of the heath back in the 1840s. It is all smart now.

The real interest lies in the church. The nineteenth century gave Surrey quite a range from the very English at Holmbury St. Mary to the Byzantine at Lower Kingswood. Here there is an imitation roadside church from the Continent, sometimes described as Italian, sometimes Spanish. The frescoes inside always make me think of Italy.

It was built in 1895 by C. Harrison Townsend who had just completed one of the notable London buildings of that period, the Bishopsgate Institute. His other notable buildings, the Whitechapel Art Gallery and the Horniman Museum were yet to come. The frescoes at Blackheath are not his work but by a Mrs Lea Merritt.

In the same year a monastery was being built at Blackheath for the Franciscans. The architect this time was F. A. Walters who built St. John's Seminary at nearby Wonersh, also in the same year. The Roman Catholic Church in Godalming is also his. For Greyfriars, here at Blackheath he did not follow the usual medieval pattern but put both the church and the dormitories all under the same roof.

26

Blechingley

➤ Sometimes you'll find this village spelled with a 't' in fourth place; even the Council once managed different spellings on different boards!

Arriving here you'll feel a sense of place for it has a great street sweeping down the hillside, widening so much there was room to build Middle Row within it, thereby creating some very attractive little side ways. Once this was an open market place overlooked by a castle on top of the hill. The castle was involved, without conflict, in the aftermath of Magna Carta and then in the troubles with Simon de Montfort for which it was destroyed in 1264. The market declined and Blechingley sank to being a 'rotten borough' until abolished by the 1832 Reform Act.

The site of the castle is worth seeing. Take the footpath on the left as you walk up to the top of the hill and it will skirt round the hillside. The castle was on the right (recently excavated) but nothing remains worth looking at except the position. It is magnificent. The downs fall away sharply into a deep deep combe with other downs folding into it, making it one of the finest downland views in Surrey. Fortunately photographs do not do it justice so it remains little publicised.

The fine church has a boring plain tomb in the south chancel arcade heralding the arrival of Renaissance design. It is of Sir Thomas Carwarden who was far from boring. He held high office for the Tudors, from Henry VIII to Elizabeth and changed his politics to suit each new monarch but without being executed. He was doubted, he was suspected, he was arrested and interrogated but dear old Thomas was a survivor.

One of his offices was Steward to Anne of Cleves at the Royal manor where she was placed. It was to the north in the vale below this high windy ridge. The manor has gone but what does remain is a magnificent half-timbered building known as Brewer Street Farmhouse. It has been described as the original gatehouse but that has been disputed. Hopefully, recent excavations will lead to a fuller understanding of the site. For now, enjoy this superb piece of craftsmanship for simply being that.

The Bourne

➤ Not just the name of a little river but also of a spread of development south of Farnham. Locally there are distinctions between Upper, Middle and Lower Bourne but collectively they insist upon the prefix 'The'.

Driving through on the main road it doesn't look much but turn off onto Vicarage Hill and it is more worthwhile. Just round the bend is a tiny burial ground on the right that's worth a look. It has long been left to nature. The skinny lime saplings once planted between the graves have flourished into sun-shattering maturity. Dribbles and splatters of sunlight splash and sparkle over the aging headstones, green with damp. Some are now completely shrouded in ivy. Other graves are shielded by rich coverings of lush polypody ferns. Primrose and woodspurge show where spring enlivens the woodland before the limes come into leaf. Where there's a gap in their canopy the puddles of sunlight send the grasses waving upwards to dry pale and gleam pale in the late summer light. On a good summer's day is the day to see it.

Vicarage Hill drops very steeply with the older homes at the top. Leading off and also very steep is Old Church Lane with a good variety of old cottages heeled into the hillside. Vine Cottage was George Sturt's, hence some of his writing under the name George Bourne. He was the man who could infect readers all over the country with his love and respect for traditional craftsmanship in his *Wheelwright's Shop*. He was the man who captured the local people, speech and customs in *Small Boy in the Sixties* and who also showed a wider intellect in his *Journals*.

In Sturt's day much of the area was not the trees of today

but hopfields and there's a reminder of that further west in Bat and Ball Lane, leading to a pub of that name. Yes, the pub has cricketing connections but before that it was the tallyman's house for the hop pickers. The fields were all around and they would bring their harvest here for assessing.

It is well and truly hidden now if you approach by Bat and Ball Lane. That becomes a footpath which falls down a long flight of steps in the steep hillside to a stream among the trees at the bottom. There you'll thankfully find the pub.

Bowlhead Green

➤ How can anywhere seem so remote in a county like Surrey? This hamlet, between Brook and Thursley, is well worth finding and the route through the country lanes is a pleasure in itself, especially from the Thursley direction.

Instead of the lanes skirting the green, they cut through, creating smaller greens and seeming to set the houses well back. What houses they are, too. Brick and tile of course but so harmonious here that it's perhaps the best place to visit to get saturated in the local style of south west Surrey. In particular note the 'hipped' roofs, i.e. the ridge is shorter than the eaves necessitating a pitch of tiles at each end instead of a gable. Note too, along the ridges, the chimneys that are offset from centre, indicating great age immediately. Three or four go back to the sixteenth century.

At the southern end is Bowlhead Green Farm. Fine in itself but for those who can read the evidence, there's plenty to reveal its internal changes since the sixteenth century. Additionally there's a good barn beside it, weatherboarded and still in use. Best of all, it is well maintained, for so many are not. Surrey is losing its farm buildings at an alarming rate, so enjoy this one while you can. The farm is still a working farm which helps to make the hamlet all the more complete.

Each of the houses has its own reward. Emley Cottage is attractive but the bricked-in round head to a window adds a

little distinction to the front. There's an old tiled roof over the well to the rear of Frith Cottage at the other end of the hamlet. Nearby, on the corner of the green is a large cottage with an odd extension with Gothic Y-tracery windows almost hidden in wisteria. It is called Chapel Cottage and there is a cross on the gable to confirm it. Evangelism arrived here about 1865 and Isaac Kettle built this chapel, promising about 1880 that he'd bequeath it to the Godalming Church group for perpetual use. When he died in 1906 he had in fact bequeathed it to a relative. That was the end of that!

Over the green is Corner Cottage, decent eighteenth century, with a blocked up window to remind us of the window tax (1696 – 1851). Forge Cottage looks a little odd; probably there's half-timbering under the outer cladding. There is only one example of black and white timbering and that's the Old Post House back up near Emley Farm. It is a grand walk round.

Bramley

➤ William the Conqueror gave Bramley to Bishop Odo and the act is commemorated in the village sign outside the library. It was carved, without the intention of it being coloured, by George Taylor, best known for his superb wildlife sculptures and past Council Member of the Society of Wildlife Artists. The sign was part of Bramley's celebrations of Queen Elizabeth's Silver Jubilee in 1977.

The rest of the village suffers from the main road and a poor sense of townscape in the centre. Each addition seems to have been made with scant concern for its place or neighbours. Thus some of the villas towards the south are overpowered yet have a simple decency worth a quick look.

Right at the south the story of the village development and sense of community is revealed by the school. The oldest part is inscribed:

> Glory to God
> Goodwill to man
> Erected 1850 for the Education
> Of the children of Poor in the
> Principals of that Branch of Christ's
> Church which is established in England
> by the widow of
> Alexander Hendras Sutherland.

Having proved its worth, the local people built on an extension. To the left is the infant school edition 'by public subscription, 1874' and then another addition:

> A 1894 D
> Erected by public subscription as a Memorial to
> Percy Ricardo Esq. VP., D.L.,
> Late of Bramley Park who died Oct 20 1892.

Within sight is East Manor House, a marvellous timber framed house that shows so much that you'll find in the textbooks: the main hall, the service passage, the cross wing, and then more behind; an impressive assertion.

Out of Bramley's jumble, to the north is the attractive green and homes of Gosden Common. The side lane runs down to the Wey Arun Junction Canal opened in 1816. A Trust is currently working to restore as much of it as possible but this stretch is still reverting to nature in a most attractive way now that the canal is disused. Next is the bridge over the railway that caused the closure of the canal. The railway itself only then lasted one hundred years.

Brockham

'History emanates from the parish pump' wrote Dr. Ralph Vaughan Williams when living near Dorking, and this Dorking village retains a pump under a little tiled roof on the edge of the green. It was erected over a long-disused spring as a memorial to Henry Hope of Betchworth Park. He had been a great Victorian benefactor to the village, most notably for giving the land beyond the green for the church.

The green is known far and wide for being used so often to illustrate the beauties of English villages. They still use photographs showing cricket on the green yet that ceased many years ago when cricket balls and car windscreens proved so incompatible. The use of the green has often been contentious. It used to be common pasture land and the villagers stubbornly continued this practice after their rights to do so had been extinguished in 1812. The vicar got so tired of the animals breaking into the churchyard that he campaigned to stop it in 1852. He wasn't very successful and so in 1868 the care of the green was put into the hands of a committee and this put an end to cattle on the green.

In more recent times the village green has won fame for the size and splendour of its celebrations on Bonfire Night.

Brockham folk come across as being a very independent lot. They walked to church in Betchworth rather than build their own, until the Lord of East Betchworth Manor collected funds to provide them with one. They were not an ungodly lot though and when in 1783 a Gospel Minister travelled from Epsom to preach he met with some success and some heckling too. Within a few months his Mission was so successful that a chapel was built. It still stands (Surrey's oldest?) set back among the lovely range of buildings along the north side of the green, backed by the line of the North Downs, patterned with woods and fields and the shadows of passing clouds. Nothing should ever be allowed to destroy such views. It is rather like Shamley Green, in not having any outstanding architecture yet when the whole village landscape is taken into account it creates something that is outstanding.

The Downs protect the Vale of Holmsdale from some of the cold north winds and so, with the good soils it is no surprise to find dozens and dozens of farms scattered all around through the Vale. They are mostly old mellowed farmhouses with traditional barns etc, unconcreted yards and little duckponds. It is everyone's idea of the countryside.

Brook

Just one row of buildings edging up to the wall of Witley Park and that is about all. Usually in Surrey such places camouflage the signs of a much earlier beginning and this is no exception. Along the row there is a black and white half-timbered building but most of the 16th–17th century homes are up on the ridge behind, called Sandhills. There are about half a dozen along the way to Witley. It was popular in the nineteenth century too; the artist Helen Allingham lived here and recorded many local scenes. Fortunately some of the books she illustrated have now been re-issued and the old scenes can be viewed again. One is of the Malt House in Brook. That is still there but it's been altered. The view to the Hindhead Hills is still there of course. Her painting of this was ridiculed for the intensity of the blue, but if you look from here in the right light, you'll see she got it absolutely correct.

Brookwood

➤ Intimidated by the spread of Woking, Brookwood is one of those places people drive through without being tempted to stop. It has tales to tell though.

If you are waiting at the central traffic lights there's the tale of the nearby canal bridge. It is one of a set rebuilt by Woking Council early this century, by an arrangement with the canal company that they would prepare the groundwork and the Council would bridge it over but at the company's expense. For that money the Council had to go to court. They won their case. Even so, they never got their money.

Just up the road, in what seems to be Knaphill, is Brookwood Hospital, well known in mental health circles. It is one of several built in Surrey as great asylums by the Victorians. This one was finished in 1881 at a cost of nearly £105,000 on land that had already cost £10,500 in 1860. It was just one of a group of great institutions hereabouts (see Knaphill for the prisons and barracks). It was all profitable business for the local brickworks.

As you might guess, the railway came through here. That was in 1839 but a station wasn't added until 1864. Ten years earlier it had become a junction with a branch line for the dead. Along this travelled the 'coffin trains' of the London Necropolis and National Mausoleum Company to their vast cemetery nearby. It's divided into two by Cemetery Pales from which road either half may be entered. There were two stations.

Catholics went to the north and Anglicans went to the south. You need an old map and the experience of an archaeological fieldwalker to discover much today but behind the long roadside walls is a weird and wonderful land rarely explored. It's hidden Surrey all right.

The south entrance leads to a winding road under mature trees sheltering masses of lesser trees and shrubs with grassy glades. Dozens of named avenues lead off either side one after another, but the view is not along streets of headstones. Those that there are totter amid long grasses where an occasional angel casts her eyes to the ground. There's a small but varied collection of more architectural memorials including a superb little Gothic chapel. That's next to the Orthodox Chapel and Shrine of St. Edward the Martyr. Nearby is the memorial to Sir Thomas Beecham, great conductor, who died in 1961. There's also a wide variety of mature conifers for the tree enthusiast.

The northern half has a totally different atmosphere. Here is the Brookwood Memorial and the War Graves revealing differences in national style. A magnificent eagle rises over the Czechoslovakian graves. Almost opposite is the American Military Cemetery, carefully landscaped and beautifully maintained. It can be approached along an avenue of Wellingtonias which is the best feature here in terms of trees. It is all surprising yet remains hidden behind its walls.

It is difficult to imagine stream trains coming here. They came from their own special station at Waterloo where the platform was divided by a screen; mourners on one side and coffins on the other. That station moved about Waterloo three times before going altogether. The last of the tracks there were removed in 1956/7.

Another railway story is indicated by two brick abutments on the north side of the railway bridge at the west end of the village street. Here crossed the old Bisley Camp Branch Line which opened in 1890. It was about a quarter of a mile long and was only used for about one month a year. Its purpose was simply to service each July the annual meeting at Bisley Camp of the National Rifle Association.

However, during the First World War it was promptly extended to the military camps at Pirbright, Deepcut and Blackdown. Up came the tracks of the extension by the early 1920s, only to be relaid as far as Pirbright during the Second World War. The line closed in 1952 leaving much of interest for the railway historian but very little for the general explorer, although the bay and unloading platform still survive at Brookwood station.

Buckland

This is the Buckland of the notorious 'Buckland Bends' that feature in too many traffic reports. The A25 slices the church away from the little green and village pond, destroying the tranquillity.

The smart little church is well worth a visit. Inside is a wooden spiral stair to the belfry just as in Capel's. Both churches were victorianised by Henry Woodyer but whereas he gave little of merit to Capel, here in 1860 he created one of his masterpieces. It is all in proportion, has the right scale, enclosing a volume that feels right and so it has the expected village church atmosphere. He retained the old timber framing of the belfry and the medieval glass and that is some of the finest fourteenth century glass we have. Two big panels remain intact opposite the south door. Dating from about 1380 one shows St. Peter, identifiable by his keys and the other is St. Paul with his sword. Further east is a super little study in silvered glass from the fifteenth century. It shows the Madonna and Child but look closely and you'll see Christ is stretching out to touch a little bird held in Mary's hand. Then in the south west chancel window are two panels showing a monk and a knight. The style is medieval but the colouring is unconvincing. It hasn't aged. The panels were actually made in 1933 to the description left by an early antiquary before the originals were lost; great idea!

Come in spring. The cherry trees in blossom make all the difference.

Burford Bridge

This spot is really part of Mickleham but the Hotel, Stepping Stones and access to Box Hill mean that it is becoming better known than the name Mickleham. Even in the eighteenth century it was popular and noisy with trippers. Nowadays it is such a popular rendezvous for motorcyclists who come in their hundreds on a Sunday afternoon that several film crews have recorded it.

The stepping stones across the river Mole have only been there since 1932 but they have already become a well-known and much photographed feature of the county. In 1946 they were renewed at the expense of Home Secretary James Chuter Ede who had Surrey connections as had the Prime Minister, Clement Attlee, who officially declared them open again.

Part of Burford Bridge Hotel is an enormous tithe barn dating from about 1600 which gives a rare opportunity to view the massive timbering of the roof of such a vernacular building. It was originally at Abinger before being dis-

mantled and brought here in 1934, complete with musicians' gallery and fireplace. Nowadays it is beautifully maintained as the banqueting hall but not officially 'open to the public'. Enthusiasts may be shown it when it is not in use, except at weekends and meal times.

Many of Mickleham's famous visitors knew this hotel. John Keats wrote part of *Endymion* and Robert Louis Stevenson wrote part of *The New Arabian Nights* here. Nelson was here to say farewell to Lady Hamilton before he left for Trafalgar. Of the lesser known associations here are members of Leslie Stephen's Society of Sunday Tramps who came to meet George Meredith for a day's rambling in the beautiful district.

Burstow

If you have memories of Greenwich Park they'll be revived here for when John Flamsteed, England's first Astronomer Royal, was not at the Royal Observatory he was making infrequent visits here as rector. There is an explanation of his life and times on the west wall, plus a plaque and a memorial window.

Burstow's other claim to fame is its timber west tower; a terrific piece of late medieval construction work. Just look at the size of the base plinths for the central construction. Notice also how the upper stages are buttressed from the ground but from outside the central structure, thus requiring the lean-to roofs that so attractively mark the stages from the outside.

Opposite the church is a little gem; a purpose built Sunday School, showing clearly its two stages of development. The earliest was built in 1859 'from the proceeds of a bazaar'. That must have been a highly profitable bazaar! The second phase was added in 1911 in memory of Edward VII and to commemorate the coronation of George V.

It is an unexpectedly attractive corner lost in the trees. Just up the lane is Moat End House and quiet waters under more trees. Follow the track to its other end and there's Gatwick House with a tower and Regency details to catch the eye.

Busbridge

◢ Once scattered over the hill above Godalming it is now rapidly becoming an extension of the town. Some of the earlier country houses are still dotted around beyond the development.

Busbridge Hall was once important but the late Palladian house was pulled down in 1906. Its successor was not built on the same site, thus isolating it from the former stables. These were then converted into Busbridge Lakes House, built with Dutch gables that were once again fashionable at the time. The lakes and grounds have survived as an important example of the landscape garden of the eighteenth century complete with many of the trimmings such as bridges, hermit's cave, grotto, pavilion etc. One of the temples was moved to Hatchlands and is therefore in the care of The National Trust. The cricket pavilion, of much later date, went on to serve as the village hall.

The Busbridge/Munstead district is famous for its connections with Gertrude Jekyll and her great friend and partner, Sir Edwin Lutyens. Her tomb, by Sir Edwin, can be found in Busbridge churchyard and both of them modified the church interior. It's the Lutyens' design for the rood screen and rood that is most likely to catch our eye, not only for being a fine piece of work from the time and part of our national collection of work from the great architect but also because it is made in wrought iron. There's little fine ironwork in Surrey. The choice of that material brought to Busbridge another great artist who made it; J. Starkie Gardner, an authority on wrought iron. It's not just the ironwork that rewards inspection but also the way it performs its function in the space provided.

Outside, one doesn't have to go far to find the views and country lanes beloved by Gertrude Jekyll, including the odd natural gorge of Thorncombe Street created along a geological fault line.

Byfleet

◣ It is easy to miss a corner where you can dream of leisurely Edwardian regattas. It is where the A245 crosses the M25 and also the Wey Navigation, hidden in the trees by the side. At this point it was broadened so that craft could turn around at what was once the wharf for the local district. It was quite an industrial scene with six grist mills, one of which remains. It's the odd brick building against the south side of the bridge. From the north side you can hire boats from a boathouse that once served the regattas. It was reserved for the less well-to-do while their superiors used the grander building opposite which has since been converted into a private house.

The medieval fenestration of the church has Y-tracery, making this the only complete church of its date in Surrey. That date has been much argued, varying from 1280 to 1310. Then in 1985 the wall painting was restored and found to be in three layers and from the details a date of 1280–90 was fixed. Other arguments were settled too. The figure is not a king after all and neither is he holding royal symbols of office, nor is the name 'Edward II' painted with it.

Byfleet is the saddest example in the county of an old village destroyed by development this century. Only names like Brewery Lane and Hopfield Avenue belie its traditional past for only one Surrey-style tile-hung cottage has survived. Other names like Edward II Avenue and Gaveston Close record the former importance of the royal manor.

Fortunately the wrangles over ownership of the village school lasted into more enlightened times. It's now been carefully redesigned and the site developed as a Day Centre for the elderly. And a super job they've made of it too. It is the best recent development (opened 1986) of this type that was found when preparing this book. Parts of the interior have not been changed much at all, which delights many of the users for they can recall their childhood days in the same building.

Nearby, the tiny fire station has survived and appears

freshly restored. Like Tongham village hall, it shows that brick doesn't have to be boring.

Capel

'These almshouses are erected to the
memory of Charles Webb of Clapham
Common Esq're by his sons and daughters'

So says the inscription below his coat of arms in the centre of a very fine range. It is mid-nineteenth century and so escaped many of the fancy details that might occur at a slightly later date. It is a low dignified building in brown stonework, worthy of Webb and his children who have had their initials incorporated: EW, TW, MW, JW and another EW.

Perhaps it looks all the more dignified because of the company it keeps. In contrast, its neighbours are bright with red tiles and white brick, twisted half timbering and all one would expect from an old Surrey village. Indeed there is a goodly total of 'listed' buildings at Capel but, oddly, there is little to arrest the eye for very long. Visually speaking, the Old Post Office/Old Stores is the most intriguing for the odd angle of junction between the two and the great chimney partially filling that junction.

The Friends' Meeting House is early, dating from 1725 but even by then Quakers had been gathering here for a long time, since the Bax family made their home the local centre from 1655. Even the founder of the movement, George Fox, came here.

The Anglican church was largely rebuilt by Henry Woodyer and it is not his best work, but there is a good tale with which to illustrate village life. Evidently when John Allen was vicar in the seventeenth century he frightened the Puritans into ejecting him on a charge of witchcraft, because he'd invented a cure for toothache. Replacing him was less easy because the villagers refused to pay their tithes until their former cleric was reinstated. He wasn't, but the fuss lasted a goodly time.

A couple of miles north up the main road, is Beare Green. There's not much to it but one building is worth a peep. It's Cherry Tree Cottage beside the footpath that leads north east off the Green. It is seventeenth century with a great end chimney. It is like so many of the other wealden buildings except that it is so very small. It's tempting but wrong to think of it as a peasant's house, for in its youth even this little home had considerable status.

Chaldon

If visiting old churches hasn't caught your imagination yet then this one will. If you want to interest the children then bring them here.

Painted all over the west wall is a great 'comic-strip' story of what will happen to us when we die if we are not good enough now. To decide that, you will find St. Michael (upper left) weighing souls, with a great devil trying to pull down the scales in his favour. Those lucky souls who weighed lightly are led across symbolic clouds to the Ladder of Salvation up which others already climb to reach Christ above.

On the right is shown the consequence of weighing heavily: Christ thrusts a devil, large with evil, down into the fires of hell. Small souls, light with goodness, rise free, worshipping Christ.

The Ladder of Salvation descends below the symbolic clouds, with condemned souls cascading down it. A devil with cloven hooves scoops them off. Some he pitches to a couple of hideous workmates behind him, who thrust them into a boiling cauldron. Behind them dancers have their feet savaged by a monster beast. Nearby, a wolf bites the hand that never offered charity.

42

Over on the right is the Tree of Knowledge complete with serpent. Beside it two great devils torment those who have committed the seven deadly sins. They seem to be walking the plank, but one so narrow they slip astride it, to come down upon vicious spikes driven up through it. They carry the symbols of their work to identify them with the medieval viewers. Clearest is the blacksmith carrying a horse-shoe in his tongs. Below, two demons force a usurer into the flames; he still has all his money bags; even his mouth spills coins.

Dating from about 1200, this is one of England's most famous wall paintings, attracting many visitors. Nevertheless, the church is well hidden among trees and fields away from the modern development of Caterham. It is well worth looking for.

Charlwood

➤ The village cage has nothing to do with its zoo and aviary. It is a prison, dating from the eighteenth century, when villages were far more self-sufficient and dealt with their own offenders. Look for a small square brick building with two small square windows – all suitably uncomfortable on a winter's night. It is in Rosemary Lane.

Not far away is a building dating from about 1800, not of brick in classical style but of cream weather boarding with simple shuttered windows. All along the front is a wide verandah just like an American 'porch' where you'd expect to find a gunslinger cooling his heels, hat down over his eyes. Modify this image to a cavalry frontier post and you won't be far wrong. The building was originally a barracks at Horsham during the Napoleonic Wars. Then in 1816 it was rebuilt here as the Providence chapel. So much for all those enthusiastic references to it being an outstanding piece of Non-Conformist pre-Wesleyan architecture! Even so, it is a rather super building.

Over in the parish church we are introduced to the Sander or Saunders family who gave their name to Sanderstead before moving to Charlwood Place by the early fourteenth century. They were a big family, repeating the Christian names, so they're not easy to sort out.

It is presumed that it was the Richard Sander who died in 1480 who was commemorated by his family with the provision of a fine parclose screen around their chapel in church. It has since been moved to act as a chancel screen but still bears the initials 'RS' in the centre of the intricately carved cresting. It is a beautiful piece of woodwork, the finest medieval screen left in Surrey, coloured and gilded afresh by William Burges in 1858. It's just the sort of job he loved and was so good at. If you've seen what he did at Castell Coch outside Cardiff then you'll know what I mean.

A particularly interesting member of the family was Thomas who presumably provided the memorial brass to his parents as he is the only child mentioned by the inscription. It records that he was the King's Remembrancer of the Exchequer and if we look closely at the brass we can see that one of the four sons shown in the background has a different costume which is probably dear Thomas showing off his official gown of office. After all, he had only got the promotion a few months before and was no doubt still proud of it.

The king he served was Edward VI but the year is 1553 so the inscription records his father's death on 29th August as being in the first year of Queen Mary's reign. What doesn't show up is the nine day reign of Lady Jane Grey between the other two monarchs. Thomas knew all about that chaos though because this was the year that he served as Sheriff of Surrey and Sussex and was thus one of the Crown's chief administrators for the county and had to deal with all the contradictions that came to him. An indication of the haste and panic at the time comes with a letter sent by the Lords of the Council on 8th July to Mr. Carden and Mr. Saunders which should have been addressed more properly to Sir Thomas Cawarden and Sir Thomas Saunders!

Chelsham

➤ Very little has survived in Surrey to show the transition from Gothic to Renaissance styles in art. Here though, the church screen does just that. Unfortunately it has been cut up and only the middle layer survives as a low chancel screen. Nevertheless it shows the usual Gothic tracery lights but instead of these being supported on mullions they have turned columns with a scaly texturing which is a Renaissance idea. The top cornice was also in Renaissance style with a frieze of heads in roundels but this has gone. The solid panels of the base were cut off too but they are made up into the chest in the vestry. A good idea of what the complete screen looked like can be seen in the reredos behind the altar which is a miniature version of it.

By the lych gate still stands the stable for visiting priests' horses, for this has always been a remote and scattered parish. Inside, the stable still comprises two stalls; perhaps the sole survivor in Surrey.

Chiddingfold

➤ This is a fine example of the settlements out in the Weald that developed into villages in the thirteenth century. It still has its church, village pond and green from that time. It rapidly grew as the centre for the surrounding industrial sites producing iron and glass. There were even glass furnaces on the village green until Elizabeth I put a stop to them. Today the village is still surrounded by little habitation groups scattered through the woods and fields. Furnace Place gives away its origins with its very name.

As the industries flourished so did local wealth, providing money enough to build with such fine timber and craftsmanship that many survive today. Most of the Surrey Wealden villages have timbered buildings going back to the sixteenth century and fewer to the fifteenth but here there are fine examples from the fourteenth century.

Most famous of these is the *Crown Inn* on the village green itself. It is so impressive it's difficult to believe it is not of a later date. So few early timber-framed houses of an impressive stature survive that it is easy to overlook how early such accommodation could be provided.

Another example with public access is the *Lythe Hill Hotel* over towards Haslemere. That's part fourteenth century, part sixteenth and once the home of the Quenells. They were important iron founders with ironworks in the parish, principally at Imbhams not far away. It's all gone now, like the rest, save the 'hammer ponds' that provided water power to drive the great hammers. There are beautiful walks to the ponds through the woods and farmlands, especially when the spring wild flowers are at their best. Beware though, it's a clay soil with glorious mud after wet weather.

All has long been quiet on the heavy industry front in this parish. It has returned to its original woodland crafts, becoming famous for its walking stick factory. Last century it was an area of deprivation like the rest of rural Surrey and as elsewhere it had good Christians who were not at one with the established Church. Here too they responded to the Baptist revival and began gathering together in someone's kitchen. In this case it was that of a farm ran by a Mr. Voller at Ramsnest, one of those little places scattered outside the village. Very soon these meetings were too popular to be accommodated around the kitchen range and they had to move out. A nearby barn was converted for their use. They had to put down their own wooden floor and put up with the rain hammering on the iron roof. For baptisms they had to dam the stream outside to make a pool suitably deep for immersions.

The meetings prospered and so did their finances. In less than ten years they were buying land nearer the village centre, in Woodside Road, to build their own proper church. That was in 1904 and it is still in use today, complete with the wooden floor that they transferred from the barn.

Chilworth

➤ Gunpowder is an unusual topic for the village explorer but Chilworth has a site of manufacture going back hundreds of years. As it persisted well into this century there are still clear signs in the woods beside the Tillingbourne: altered water courses, ruined buildings, lengths of railway track, crushing stones and several craters from unfortunate incidents. All can be traced using *A Guide to the Chilworth Gunpowder Mills* by Glenys Crocker (Surrey Industrial History Group).

Enriching the site even further are the remains of a paper-making industry but exploding gunpowder filling the air with burning debris was not compatible with paper

making and so the latter moved out. Unwins moved their business to the mill at Old Woking and still flourish there today, as printers rather than paper makers.

The industrial sites are best reached off Halfpenny Lane. The origin of that odd name, I'm told, is that it was the toll levied on the cattle drovers using it as a short cut to Guildford market over the hill.

The house and gardens of Chilworth Manor are regularly opened to the public. The manor goes back to medieval times and the gardens include a fine range of terraces on the hillside illustrating taste and design from the seventeenth century. The walled garden was added in the eighteenth century for Sarah, Duchess of Marlborough. The house follows the same pattern; basically seventeenth century with an additional eighteenth century wing. When it is opened flower decorations provided by local floral art groups enhance the house still further.

Chipstead

You can't imagine the difference between the two Chipsteads. Down in the Valley I was told 'You'll need an earthquake to make this place interesting' and they were right.

Old Chipstead, however, is high on the Downs above; a country of close hedged lanes, masses of trees and small fields tilting in all directions over the undulations. There's a goodly scattering of large modern country houses, a few old ones, and not a great deal more. There's a good group by the school.

To the south is Elmore Pond by the road and turning east here, along Elmore Road brings you up to the isolated church which looks on the map as though it's Hooley's. The situation is pleasing up on the skyline with a smart little green in front. Usually it is locked but I remember interesting Victorian glass in the east window and a good but simple medieval screen. Outside, the west doorway was built of chalk and has weathered badly. It looks at first glance like Perpendicular work but its pretty but fussy detail belies the much later date of 1883. It is by Norman Shaw, better known for his domestic houses. It is part of a fine cruciform church of the thirteenth century of which the fenestration is particularly fine (beware, though, for the southern windows are replacements).

In the churchyard there is an imposing avenue of large Irish yews which no longer bear any relation to the design of the churchyard. It would be interesting to know the story behind this.

Chobham

◢ Come in spring when the banks of the street-side stream are rich with daffodils. It is one of Surrey's finest village streets with Sundial House, thought to be the oldest timber-framed house in the County (13th century). It's been altered over the centuries so outwardly it doesn't look so ancient.

Nearby is a patch of grass, fondly called the village green in one book, on which a cannon stands. It's a real one. Back in 1901 it was drawn into the village by four hundred children to record a visit by Queen Victoria to review her troops in 1853. It was a Russian twenty-four pounder captured in the Crimean War but alas in 1942 it had to be melted down to help the war effort in the Second World War. Then in 1979 it was replaced with one on loan from a museum, on a modern carriage that was made locally.

This seems an unlikely place to find an Archbishop of York, but Queen Mary Tudor sold Nicholas Heath the manor for £3,000. Here he died but his memorial is nothing more grand than the plain blue marble slab on the church floor.

When he was Bishop of Worcester he refused to take the

oath under Henry VIII's Act of Supremacy and he went on to refuse later reforms under Edward VI, such as replacing altars with communion tables. For this he was put away in the Tower of London. His diocese was put in the care of John Hooper but when Catholic Mary Tudor came to the throne there were further religious upheavals during which she had John Hooper burned, at Gloucester. She reinstated Nicholas Heath into his bishopric from where he went on to be Archbishop and then Lord Chancellor. It was he who proclaimed Elizabeth to be the new queen upon the death of Mary. Elizabeth I was a Protestant and required of Nicholas an oath for the Second Act of Supremacy making her Supreme Head of the Church in England. No such oath was forthcoming so Nicholas went to the Tower again. Eventually he was allowed to retire here and it is even said that Elizabeth ignored the fact that he was apparently celebrating the Roman Catholic mass in his own private chapel in Chobham Park. Indeed her respect for him was such that on more than one occasion she visited him in his retirement.

Outside the village centre are some fine farmhouses. One pleasant corner is left off the Woking road, up Philpott Lane to a humped bridge and the eighteenth century Emmetts Mill. That's best seen when the leaves are off the trees. Past the Victorian letterbox and round the corner is Brooklands House. It's really smart with walls chequered in pink and grey brick, beautifully proportioned as we'd expect from the eighteenth century. There's no austerity, just a dignified homeliness. Next door is a tiny cottage from the previous century, with black beams and brick infill. Not to be outdone by its neighbour, it was given a brick facade – not very proficiently; see how it niggles over the jetty.

Churt

The cleverest thing about Churt is the way the centre clusters around the crossroads, looking completely attractive, and yet composed of nothing particularly attractive at all.

Odd is the way the village green, not of great age, is flung over a ridge so that the centre is the highest point. Thus the few buildings and the main road are all looked down upon. This includes the church, built by Ewan Christian who put the pinnacles on Farnham church. This is simpler and far more attractive than some of his work. In the south transept hangs a large wooden crucifix made up of wooden blocks, jig-saw fashion.

Nearby is Croft Cottage, simple and pleasing sounding as though it should be out on a heath. It once was. See the heather and gorse fighting the grass to regain their place on what is now the green.

Another nearby house is Redhearn which was the village bakery until quite recently. A second old bakehouse stands in Hammer Lane. There's the Old Forge and Old Kiln too. Such self-sufficiency seems odd now with the main road destroying all sense of remoteness.

Cobham

The village is of two parts, Street Cobham (the old A3, now A307) and Church Cobham, linked by Between Streets.

Firstly, Street Cobham. 'The first bridge on this site was built about the year 1100 by Queen Matilda, wife of King Henry I as an act of charity in consequence of the drowning of one of her maidens at the ford.' So reads a stone on the 'upstream' parapet of the modern bridge over the river Mole. Evidently there is no documentary evidence for this eventful day when the royal court set out from Stoke D'Abernon manor. It is part of Surrey's oral tradition.

On one bank is Matthew Arnold Close built on the site of Painshill Cottage and garden where Matthew Arnold (see Laleham) lived from 1873 until his sudden death in 1888. From here he wrote sensitive descriptions of the Surrey countryside and his pets, and much enjoyed gardening.

On the other bank is Painshill Park, now being restored and regularly open to the public. Beyond that, along the Byfleet Road is a cemetery for pets, one of so few of its kind in the country. Surely Matthew Arnold would have approved! Opposite are the flanks of St. George's Hill on which Gerard Winstanley and the Diggers created allotments in 1650. They were a less political wing of the Levellers. Their cause was to abandon the idea of owning property and to give everything over to the common people. Certainly their little vegetable patches, which must have inspired the same unease as Communism can do today, soon drew the attention of Lord General Fairfax and the Officers of the Parliamentary army. After much debate the Diggers were evicted.

Between Streets begins with a terrace of white cottages called Post Boys Row. Here I'm told is where such people were accommodated when the mail coaches stopped at the inn opposite. Despite being called boys these were usually grown men, aging even!

The first mail coach ran in Britain in 1797 after a wrangle between the Prime Minister and the Post Master, which the former won. The services continued until 1847 when most were transferred onto the railways.

Church Cobham has had most of its main street gutted and rebuilt as modern shops, yet it is worth an overall look. It has cleverly kept a sense of place partly by the enclosing feel of the tallish buildings and by the turn of the road at each end. It's a busy place too which keeps it feeling alive and is one of the few places I'd recommend visiting during shopping hours.

Two recent buildings are worth a closer look and both are towards Between Streets. One is the Roman Catholic church. It is large and in some ways rather un-churchlike yet it has a stature and sense of self-possession that lifts it above the everyday, as indeed a church should. It's far superior to some of the cringing efforts provided on housing estates. This one stands in dignified isolation but gives the impression that if the development eventually creeps around then it will hold its own quite purposefully.

Looking back to the main road from here is a good viewpoint for the other building I like which happens to be a supermarket. This one is sufficiently new to be out of the phase of flat-roofed concrete and glass boxes. It has traditional tiles roofs which harmonise with its setting and it is also kept low. Best of all the basic box concept has been multiplied up into a more complex plan of rectangles. It thereby banishes the usual sense of austere squareness and creates a modern version of the sort of angled building we're familiar and happy with. It suits Cobham and it suits us – at least it suits me! Two other variants of this design have been built in the county so maybe it is something we shall become more familiar with.

At Church Cobham, Church Street retains some attractive buildings all the way down to Church Stile House which is a rarity in Surrey for having *two* projecting floors (see White Hart Cottage, Compton and the White Hart, Godalming). The Norman church, heavily Victorianised, contains two interesting brasses.

When Cobham was owned by Chertsey Abbey the local administrator was the bailiff. James Sutton was one such bailiff. There was once a memorial brass to him and his wife, Maud, in the church because historians found the inscription loose in a chest. Some say it belongs with the brass of an armoured knight that can still be seen. However, James Sutton's inscription bears the date 1530 which is twenty years too early for the details of the armour on the brass. So who is this knight?

He may well be George Bigley whose will was proved in 1558. In it he wishes to have a memorial brass. As it happens he too was bailiff, but by now the Crown held the manor following the Dissolution of Chertsey Abbey in 1537. As it also happens these two gentlemen were related. When James Sutton's son Richard died, his widow took George Bigley as her second husband. George got the bailiff's job back after Richard had followed in his father's footsteps, only to have it confiscated at the Dissolution.

More intriguing is the brass itself. It's a palimpsest. In

other words both sides have been used. To save money, the knight's image was engraved on the back of a priest's brass of about 1510. Here we have the rare chance to see both sides because it is now fixed on a rotating pivot. Thus we can see how the knight had to be the same size as the priest and more or less the same outline. Nevertheless, the priest has been snipped about a bit. Turn the pivot and see.

On the south chancel wall is another rare brass, so small it's easily missed. It shows the Adoration of the Shepherds at the Nativity. It's the only one of its kind and one of only two Bible scenes to be engraved in brass. The other is also in Surrey, at Cranleigh.

This one is the traditional scene with the ox and donkey shown in the background. They're not mentioned in the Bible though, yet they have appeared in this scene throughout Christendom for centuries. It has been suggested that at some early date it was deemed unseemly for the Son of God to lie with animals and so the early reference was edited out.

Coldharbour

➤ Leith Hill as an Area of Outstanding Natural Beauty attracts thousands of visitors every year and this is one of their favourite villages. From the surrounding hillsides there are great vistas out over the Weald and also inland towards the North Downs. Additionally there are spots from where the view shows the village of Coldharbour as a small settlement in a clearing cut out of the woodland. Several of the homes go back to the seventeenth century but it's the setting that is impressive here, not the components of the village.

Unexpectedly it has a large church, a Victorian one by Benjamin Ferrey (1848) who did a lot of work in Surrey. There is some startling colouring on the modern memorial window with orange, scarlet and crimson all blazing together. It shows St. Francis among local rhododendrons and some distinctly non-local birds. The pulpit is well-carved but the design makes it look as though it's collapsing!

Ramble on the nearby promontory and you'll find Anstiebury Camp. It is one of the largest hill forts in Surrey, covering over eleven acres within triple banks and ditches except where the scarp is so steep they weren't needed. Dating from the Iron Age it was probably in use in the first and second centuries A.D. although I'm told that during the Napoleonic Wars villagers were told to shelter there in the event of an emergency.

Compton

━━ This village is famed for its Norman church with unique two storey chancel, the Watts Chapel and Art Gallery and its downland setting with the Hog's Back running along behind.

Take the footpath next to the pub in the main street and it will lead you up into the fields over the hillside with wide views all around and the long village street in the trees below. The roofs and chimneys of a large house are immediately below. This is Field Place, sounding so innocent yet once a seat of treachery.

It's an ancient site. Field comes from felled from when the Saxons cleared the trees to make the site in the forest. The medieval habitation platform still shows in the levels of the lawns and the ornamental water is part of the old moat. Here lived Sir Thomas St. Leger, brother-in-law of King Richard III but no friend. Sir Thomas was the leader of the Surrey insurgents when they planned insurrection. At the time he slipped away to the West Country where his wife was Duchess of Exeter and where he was beheaded for treason when the uprising failed.

An attempt to found a thriving non-Conformist movement here also failed. They got as far as providing a little chapel but that is now a private dwelling and speaks for itself. Of the other interesting buildings in the street, note White Hart Cottage by the church. When it was built in the sixteenth century they obviously intended it to last. Whereas so many had no proper foundations this timber framing was anchored on a substantial stone-built base which has held it stable ever since. Even more notable is the way both the upper floors project. Buildings with two tiers of oversailing are rare in Surrey (see White Hart, Godalming High Street and Church Stile House, Cobham).

Nearby is the church, packed with interest but note also the great cedar trees over the churchyard wall. They are among the finest in England.

Crowhurst

Famous for Crowhurst Place of the Gaynesford family and for the yew in the churchyard, but have a look at Mansion House Farm opposite the church. It seems a very complicated structure, largely dating from the sixteenth century, presenting a wide frontage to the lane but also seen to be running back deeply on its site. Then in the mid-seventeenth century when brick was high fashion, a facade was built over the front elevation. All the irregularities of design of the half-timbering behind and of the fenestration prevent this being a boring brick surface, especially with its little brick gables and distinctive porch. There's something about this building that catches yet eludes the eye in a way the others do not and there are several hundred of them in Surrey.

Deepcut

◣ Through here the waters of the Basingstoke Canal surge through no less than fifteen locks, hence the name Deepcut. Obviously these posed an enormous challenge to the restorers but not an impossible one. In October 1977 six hundred volunteers arrived from all over the country for the 'Deepcut Dig' and achieved results equal to a year's work. Their work was valued at £8,000 but even so, was only part of a long-term task. In 1979 Shell UK gave a boost of £250 towards rebuilding the Lower Wilderness Weir and so on, as the dedication of the volunteer restorers continued to inspire. In some ways it's a pity that the finished sections give no indication of the astounding success stories they represent. A single lock can take 40,000 bricks. That's an awful lot of bricklaying and a lock isn't simply bricks. New gates aren't the easiest things to manoeuvre into place, let alone the raising of £25,000 to pay for a bottom pair.

Avoid seeking the towpath by crossing Pirbright Camp because some of the roads shown on the maps are closed to civilians. The housing estates for the military look exactly what they are. There is yellow brick so alien to this part of Surrey, with black weatherboarding not used in Surrey since the seventeenth century. Some of the older architecture, long and low over flat spaces has a certain bleak individuality that will catch the eye of some people.

Two roadside churches are shown on the OS Map at Deepcut. The southernmost is the garrison Church of St. Barbara; an unusual dedication in Surrey. It is large, of corrugated iron painted white. Wooden frames are black while the roof and bell turret are 'army green'. It's well lit with 'Churchwarden Gothic' windows, some with stained glass, clerestory and dormers too. It is not great architecture but at least it's individual.

Its northern neighbour is also white but of weatherboarding, with squared domestic leaded windows.

The reservation of the surrounding countryside for Ministry of Defence purposes has preserved some beautiful Surrey woods and heathland.

Dunsfold

━━ Dunsfold is one of Surrey's scattered villages. Don't look for a nucleus of old buildings, not even around the church, remote on the slopes above the infant river Arun. The road up to it is still a country lane complete with spring's wild flowers.

More than a little royal influence has come this way to create the church. Its design was ahead of its time and its workmanship of the highest standard. It dates from the late thirteenth century when experiments were made with larger windows and with grouping the openings together. This church shows one such experiment, one that earned approval and went on to be used nationally. There is only one other church in Surrey of this time. It's at Byfleet but there the experiment was totally different, introducing Y-tracery. Dunsfold's church was also provided with benches in the nave. We expect seating today but this did not become general until the fifteenth century (examples at Pyrford). Thus these at Dunsfold from c.1280 are exceptionally early – the earliest surviving set in Britain. Note the holes in the ends to take the candle prickets.

Walk down below the church to the Holy Well; few of these survive in Surrey to mark the ancient religious sites. Walk on through the fields by the footpath along the river bank to the attractive old texture brickwork of the mill. It is still unspoiled; it's like a walk through an old Victorian painting. The same can be said for the long, long, village green; so rough and wild that it is hardly recognisable as a village green. It is difficult to accept that this was once part of a heavy industry region, with glass furnaces and iron works, noise and smoke and so many of the trees consumed as fuel.

If you want a particular point of interest then look carefully around the church walls at floor level and you will find the drain holes with wooden plugs used when the floor was washed down. If you'd like something more romantic than drains then there is the story I was told twenty years ago –

that when the Commissioners during the Reformation arrived to seize the church plate and other valuables they were cheated. The villagers had buried it and it has never been found. Such stories abound but perhaps it is true. What a find it would make!

Eashing

➤ Well known for its early medieval bridge (see Tilford) and nearby cottages, it's a tranquil spot without much traffic. It is also one of the pioneering efforts at preservation, for it was given to The National Trust as early as 1901, not by a far-seeing individual but by the Old Guildford Society who were already watching much destruction in Guildford itself.

Other early organisations were at work too. It was the West Surrey Society and Thackeray Turner who gave the nearby cottages to the Trust in 1922. They were repaired in memory of Turner who had already given 240 acres of Witley and Milford Commons to the National Trust. He was an architect, taking inspiration from Voysey but with a greater sense of locality so he was more inclined to use traditional local materials; see for example the home he built for himself, Westbrook beyond the Meath Home at Godalming.

At Eashing nothing seems to change. Perhaps that's why the non-Conformist movement failed. Their chapel is now a wooden shed in the bank, I am told. At the turn of the century visitors found the riversides a mass of pink from 'beds of pink blossomed rushes' (Butomus). They are all gone and although once common (first recorded in 1597) they are now a rarity in Surrey.

East Clandon

➤ For anyone interested in village development this is a good place to visit in conjunction with nearby East Horsley.

61

The latter is predominantly nineteenth century whereas East Clandon offers a score or more buildings from the seventeenth century. Most are squidged together around the church. There is definitely a village centre leaving us to simply imagine away the metalled roads and picture a sweeping landscape of fields around and sloping up to the Downs; not too difficult.

The houses are mostly half-timbered and in-filled with brick. Opposite the church there is a good example dating from about 1690. To the left is another, Lamp Cottage, with added interest as it was built end-on to the lane so we can see both faces. The lower stages incorporate flint and some of the panels are whitened. Being end-on is not odd. Excavation of early habitation sites has revealed that periodically the house was pulled down and rebuilt on a different orientation. This just happens to be the latest position.

The medieval church hasn't anything special to offer. One tablet is very worthy. It commemorates Catharine Sumner who died in 1777. Usually at this time such a list of virtues is recorded that it is difficult to believe the person was as perfect as we are supposed to believe. This one is different. It simply says: 'Those exemplary virtues which as a daughter, wife, parent, and friend distinguished and endeared her living are worthy of remembrance and imitation.'

East Horsley

➤ A quick walk along this street leaves the visitor in no doubt that it was remodelled in the nineteenth century, primarily 1856–1867. It is not, however, one of those precious-pretty estate villages. On the contrary, it is quite stark. It is not piecemeal development either. Very clearly it is the work of one mind that has stamped its presence everywhere. Heraldic devices are sculpted into the bricks, big and self-assured. They stamp their identify into building after building, quite exciting at first but then repetitively boring. The same continuity is carried through into boundary and garden walls, even the churchyard wall. They are red and rich and quite wonderful. It's not all brick though. There's masses of flintwork too from the local building tradition that stretches right back to pre-history when the Neolithic people had flint mines here. The nineteenth century contribution is hard, flat and lacking in individuality. It was used more as a foil for the decorative brickwork rather than as a medium for exploration in its own right. It was all due to the Lords of the Manor. They were the Earls of Lovelace, residing here from 1846–1919. Their estate entrance 'must be one of the most sensational in England' said Ian Nairn.

The sequence can be ascertained from the date stones on the buildings and can be quite fun: the Red Roses 1867; Sortor Ve Sartus 1866; Bishopsgate Lodge, 1860; The School 1860, and so on. What a great building site this must have been. We're used to that from our modern estates but it must have been quite impressive to the Victorian villagers. They couldn't have been left in any doubt as to the power of their manorial lord.

There's a lovely story that the youngest choirboy would have to act as lookout from the churchyard gazebo for the Lovelaces' approach. Then he'd nip back and alert the Rector who could then adjust the proceedings to ensure they arrived with perfect timing.

Long before the Lovelaces, the lords of the manor were the Bishops of Exeter and there is an important memorial brass to one of them. He was John Bowthe, Bishop from 1465 until he died on April 5th, 1478 during a visit to the Manor of East Horsley. The brass has been cited as the one that shows more of a back view than any other. That's rubbish. The figure is in strict profile. What can be seen is the orphrey of the chasuble hanging down his back plus of course a side view of how the vestments were worn. Nowhere else can this be seen so it is very valuable to the costume experts. If you look for this as a book illustration – beware. For some reason this brass has been reproduced very inaccurately, even to the extent of placing an imaginary book in his praying hands. Come and see the real thing and you will also be viewing the only old brass to show a cleric kneeling.

A previous Bishop was Thomas de Brantyngham (1370–94) and when his brother Robert came up from his Devon Manor on a visit he too died. His memorial brass is only a half effigy of c.1390 and not especially interesting. Robert was though. When he arrived in the village he brought the prestige of being a royal servant, having been Treasurer to Edward III and then Lord Treasurer of England for Richard II.

Yet another royal servant lies with his wife on Surrey's finest table tomb monument. It is of alabaster. He is Thomas Cornwallis, 'sometimes pensioner and groome porter unto Queen Elizabeth of blessed memory'. Among his duties were those of providing cards and dice for the royal court and then to referee the ensuing arguments. His wife has the distinction of appearing on two tombs. Firstly, she appears among her siblings on her parents' tomb at Titchfield, Hants and then again here in her own right.

East Molesey

➤ Going to Hampton Court Palace? Fine – but do step across the bridge into one of two conservation areas in East Molesey. Clear your mind of Tudors and the Renaissance and think Victorian. No, you'll not find a grid of mean Victorian terraces at all. Walk up Palace Road, Wolsey Road or Arnison Road into Church Road and there's a very different type of nineteenth century development.

Some 300 acres were bought by Francis Jackson Kent and son who developed the site, principally between 1847–50. Their houses are those with classical tendencies, mostly in pale yellow brick with heavy white ornament along eaves and at all edges, whether quoins, doorways or windows. The roofs are of slate (the railway had newly arrived). The houses are generously spaced, not because so many are now missing but because they had such big gardens. Many of the saplings planted then have matured into fine trees. There are cedars of course but also sweet chestnut, horse chestnut, etc.

This is 'Kent Town' and was a private estate. The former lodge is No. 1. Palace Road. Much infilling has taken place this century which has created variety but looking at the original housing reveals considerable variation although they are all recognisable. Presumably this resulted from the building plots being sold off rather than the finished house. A vast profit was made in this way (nearly £4,000 per acre!). No wonder Kent could afford to build St. Paul's church at his own expense. He intended it to become the parish church as the old one was always so overcrowded but his offer was refused. This was a bit unfortunate but he applied to the Ecclesiastical Commissioners for permission to open St. Paul's as a district church. He offered himself as Patron. The offers were accepted. It opened on February 24th, 1856 but Bishop Sumner of Winchester didn't consecrate it until the October (30th).

It would be nice if this church could give us an idea of what Kent thought fitting for a place of worship for the people of his new estate. Ironically it was too small. A south aisle had to be added 1861–2 and a north aisle in 1864. By 1870 his nave had to be extended. Finally the present tower was added in 1887–8. This was a royal occasion, commemorated by a stone (Princess Frederica recurs elsewhere in East Molesey's history).

The church forms an island with Kent's roads knotting themselves into it with subtle rounded bends; no harsh grid here. Walking back to the town centre, notice not just the modern infilling but, tucked away, the creation of homes out of former coach houses and stables. Some are very attractive indeed. Spot the influences too; a hint of Venice here and a French roof there or iron-framed conservatories recalling the Crystal Palace and the Great Exhibition of 1851.

The shopping area is not without interest either. The Post

Office in Bridge Road catches the eye. It is a grand little red brick effort of 1906 in the Dutch gable design expected of that date. As a purpose-built Post Office it must surely be one of the earliest in Surrey. Earlier the post offices shared other premises just as East Molesey's was in a shop near the Albion, from 1867. Before that it was in *The Bell*. Dating from about 1550, *The Bell* returns us to Tudor thoughts and passing trade connected with the great palace just over the bridge.

Effingham

Surrey's greatest bishop was William of Wykeham who began building Winchester College in 1387. That didn't take all his attention though. As bishop he toured the diocese and was currently inspecting the churches in the care of Merton Priory. He found them in sad disrepair and ordered immediate repairs. One of these was the parish church of Effingham.

Thus we know from documentary evidence the exact date of the remodelling of the north and south windows of the chancel. Inevitably it was the chancel because the clergy were reponsible for that and the parishioners for the nave. That those windows were remodelled is in no doubt because nothing like them had been seen except in the new building works at Winchester College. The new design was developed there and they are still called 'Winchester Windows' today. The style is called 'Perpendicular' and according to the experts is the only contribution that England has made to the world history of art.

What isn't known is how the design actually got here in 1388. Perhaps Bishop William sent a man to do the job. It's certainly fine workmanship so it is unlikely a local builder was sent to learn at Winchester. Drawn plans do not seem to have been in use at that date but templates could have been. If full size, the cut stones would have been laid out on one to

check accuracy before erection. Somehow or other the design arrived and helped set a new architectural trend.

Effingham is a name learnt in connection with the Spanish Armada when the victorious Lord High Admiral was Charles, Baron Howard of Effingham. He went on to fight with Essex at Cadiz and was later a Commissioner at the trial of Essex, of Mary Queen of Scots and also of the Gunpowder Plot Conspirators. It was his father however, William the first baron, who was raised to the peerage, for his defence of London against Wyatt's Rebellion of 1544.

Elstead

The thing to see here is a tree. It is the Cedar of Lebanon that was planted in the churchyard in 1849 following a collection made in the church in thanksgiving for deliverance from an outbreak of cholera. What is so special about it is simply that the lower branches have not been lopped off to leave the familiar umbrella. Instead they sweep down low over the headstones, showing the real beauty of the tree. This also means that catkin-flowers and developing cones are within reach and provide a rare opportunity for inspection.

At the other extreme is the humble carrot. Elstead has a long tradition for growing these. There are records from the sixteenth century so they were quick off the mark as it is thought they were not introduced until the reign of Elizabeth I. We don't know what status they had reached by 1801 because the crop census conducted that year simply didn't ask for any carrot statistics. By this century, however, they were important. Washed and packed locally, carrots were despatched to Covent Garden via Milford Station

Elstead has developed where the heathlands shamble down to the more fertile valley of the Wey. The river is crossed by two narrow bridges parallel to each other. One is sixteenth century with a Victorian brick parapet. The other was thrown across as a 'temporary' measure during the Second World War and is still serving its purpose. At that time Sir Winston Churchill and General de Gaulle came here to watch a demonstration of a sort of tank with a front that opened out to form a bridge.

The nearby mill also has military connections for here they produced the gold braid (worsted fringe) for officers' uniforms. Before that it produced worsted cloth. Contrary to popular belief it was not a paper mill.

Opposite are rural scenes over the water meadows; such an English scene, yet one that is vanishing rapidly under modern land management. These Thundry Meadows are in the care of the Surrey Wildlife Trust to preserve their rich flora and associated butterflies etc. They too, own the beef cattle that are rotated around the grazing as of old. (Access is limited to members only). In 1986 there was only one other such site in Surrey that was being preserved – by the National Trust.

Englefield Green

➤ Horatio Nelson is buried here. His surname was Harris, and the headstone can be spotted from the path round the west end of the church. Directions are needed because the enormous churchyard has an incredible number of grave markers of all types. It reflects the above average affluence of Victorian Englefield Green, inseparable from the development of the village, arising from its proximity to the Royal Court at Windsor. The first reminder of that is right inside the gate where two little buildings stand side by side with high rising pyramids of slate as roofs. They are mausoleums of the Somersets.

The village is the best place in the region to see Victorian housing, following on in time from those noted in East Molesey.

Opposite the church is a row of shops and those at the north end (corner of Alexandra Road), were once cottages. They are dated 1865/68 and are the earliest convenient for this short perambulation. Their frontage is broad, a feature which does not recur until the end of the century. Note how each block was once two 'semis' with the shop front now destroying the twin central doors. The wall above is a blank broad space where presumably the stairs came up.

Turning into Alexandra Road one finds a superb succession beginning with Stoke Cottages. They are all yellow brick, no red, and retain their original square chimney pots with panelled sides. Opposite is Ashton Place of 1874 with narrow bay windows emerging. Red brick has been introduced to decorate the yellow. Best are those employing a soft red brick for this purpose but for a sharper contrast hard red ones were used, as in Yew Tree Cottages (1878) opposite. This does not seem to depend upon date because next comes Rose Cottage of 1893 which is back to soft red. Here however, the whole home is of red brick (but with yellow chimney pots). Incidentally, the right hand chimney stack of Yew Tree Cottages is actually signed. The corner chimney has the refinement of a band of cord decoration. A larger detail is the doorway. It is at an angle. Was this once a shop?

69

Moving on to Warwick Cottages we are back to an early phase – 1868. The lintels have prominent keystones but they are no guide to dating because they recur at nearby Weston Cottages of 1893. These, however, have little refinements such as arched doorways and a chamfered edge to the lintels. Hope Terrace was no doubt much more expensive as that has cellars – see the windows.

Alexandra Place is 1880 with red brick arched windows and more expansive bays than noted earlier. Notice that access to the shared back yard is tunnelled through the block. Further on we reach the younger houses, from the turn of the century; all red brick now and back to broader proportions.

Turn right into South Road to return to St. Jude's Road where the walk began. If, however, you want to see the sort of home built before this building boom, turn left down St. Jude's Road to Acacia Place, dated 1822 and signed 'IM'. It's deeper than the later ones. Nearby are even more variations; double ornamental courses between floors or chequered courses or courses deeply imprinted with a scallop shell motif. Lintels ornamented in relief now appear too. Further on, over the traffic lights is a new entrance to the Royal Holloway College. It yields a very good view of this famous and enormous example of Victorian architecture, inspired by the Loire's Chateau Chambord.

In St. Jude's Road, a little further north from the starting point are Melrose Cottages. These are interesting because they are of two phases, dated 1875 and 1879, but with the second phase red brick has been incorporated to decorate the yellow.

Round the corner in Bond Street is further evidence of the age of mass production. Paxton Villas, 1881, of yellow brick is relieved with a course of red nailhead above another red band impressed with a floral design in deep relief. Turning back, Hardwick Lodge, 1875, is in contrast to many seen for expressing such plain decent simplicity so demurely yet with dignity. It had a large garden (a lane runs down the side) and at the bottom an old building which was presumably for the stable/carriage. Beside it, an iron bollard is presumably the base of an early street lamp. It's marked 'Adams Ltd. York'. Beyond is modern housing in matching yellow and red brick, thank goodness.

Now for the church. That will get you totally confused viewing it from the street. E. B. Lamb (1859) had fun here breaking with convention. The tower is over the south transept so what looks like the nave is the chancel and the nave stretches back out of sight. It makes sense from the south side. It's good too. The stonework is smart and even but not monotonous, the window tracery 'Flamboyant" with an unexpected roundel at the west end. Even more surprising is the range of dormer windows just above the eaves but not breaking them. They're not 'church' windows but homely domestic ones. The overall long low proportions are very pleasing. They're so noticeable because there's no south door to interrupt the run of the eye.

Another surprise is the tower. As the eye runs up, the top masonry prepares for a stone spire but there isn't one. There isn't anything. It all sounds rather odd but in reality there is a reassuring harmony. In no way does it prepare you for the astonishing polychrome patterning of the interior.

Ewell

➤ Courtesy to one's neighbours has a tangible monument here. Walk into Spring Street and follow the garden wall of Bourne Hall and it will suddenly bow inwards. That was to allay the fears of the owner opposite who realised that the wall would not give him room to swing his carriage into his drive. A quiet word at Bourne Hall and the problem was solved.

Spring House in Spring Street is intriguing. It looks as though it's brick, at a glance, but closer inspection of the top right of the central canting reveals it is made of 'mathematical tiles' or 'brick tiles' used as a cheaper substitute for brick.

71

Cemented in, they are usually indistinguishable from brick so it is rare to be able to see them for certain. With the introduction of the brick tax in 1784 they became more popular but this house is some forty years earlier.

The springs pour down into the lake in the grounds of the former Bourne Hall. The gardens, richly planted with trees and shrubs have public access. I would rate this highest among Surrey's municipal parks. There's a small iron waterwheel to seek out by the waterside. Beyond, the waters (Hogsmill River) flow into a long mill pond reflecting the yellow brick gables of the mill. Walk round to the other side and the mill is white weatherboarded.

There's so much to see here in so small a place. It is most rewarding, but best to explore on a Sunday when there is less traffic. There is good scale and harmony with the exception of a projecting purblish brick addition by the Bourne Hall gateway. It is the wrong style, wrong materials, wrong scale, and in the wrong place, so it probably won an award!

For a more detailed look, Church Street is the best. It even has a few proper paving stones left. Many of the houses are 'listed' and create an attractive narrow street of great variety, all the better for its slope. For a simple dignified little town house how about No. 3? In red brick are Nos. 6 & 7 opposite each other and then No. 10 with its fine Tuscan porch sheltering not one door but two, set into a rusticated wall. A pyramidal roof on a low tower over the garden wall catches the eye. It is part of the old rectory, now Glyn House, in soft pinkish brick. Coming into view is Ewell Castle, a great Regency crenellated house that doesn't look out of scale simply because this end of the street has more space to take it. Opposite is another surprise for the rough churchyard with sculpted headstones doesn't contain the church, not now anyway. Only the late medieval tower stands in pre-served isolation.

The new church (1848) is further round the corner and shelters items such as brasses and the font from the old church. Best is the medieval screen. There are only a few complete examples left in Surrey but this (and Lingfield's) has the distinction of little carved dragon heads on the finials of the muntins. These are the only examples I have been able to trace of the skill and imagination of some long forgotten craftsman.

The Lord Mayor of London (1717) props himself up behind; in marble of course. He is Sir William Lewen who died in 1721. The monument is of high quality but the figure is particularly good. Although he looks as though he's carefully keeping still for the artist he also looks as though he might stretch himself and get up at any moment; a clever balance. There on his chain of office hangs the Tudor portcullis, taken by Henry VII from the arms of his mother, Margaret Beaufort, Lady of the Manor of Woking.

Ewhurst

◀ Nobody wants to put a date to the church font. It has the size and proportions to support a Norman date to match this beautiful and architecturally important Norman church but the carvings seem to deny this. I'll stick my neck out and suggest it was Norman until exiled from the church by the Puritans. When it was possible to reinstate it the Norman carving was cut back to remove the Roman Catholic associations and were replaced by the present bold unfamiliar designs.

From curiosity to beauty – how handsome is the seventeenth century woodwork of the altar rails with their spiralled balusters and recessed curved corners. They protect the altar (originally from dogs) on three sides which is uncommon. No Surrey church can match these but then they weren't for a parish church but came from Baynards Park over near Cranleigh. The somewhat earlier pulpit looks very demure in comparison.

The village outside is disappointing. There's not much of the usual Surrey style vernacular to get bored with. The houses either side of the church entrance are fun, one showing its age, the other in disguise. The grouping at the little Bull's Head Green is also worth a pause. Most of the buildings of note are scattered through the surrounding woods and fields.

Farleigh

If we could go back to Norman times we'd find many places in Surrey consisted of a large farm, a few workers' cottages and their little church. Only Farleigh in the east and Wisley in the west have remained like that. The farm and the short cul-de-sac of homes (like Betchworth) contain recent replacements but the little Norman church is almost as it was built. The chancel was altered in the thirteenth century and some restoration was necessary last century but otherwise it's as close to the original as we will find. This is especially so when the nature of the setting is taken into account.

To the west are wild and weedy commons high on the downs, all fresh air and wild flowers. There are glimpses too of a high brick tower. It belongs to a lunatic asylum built in 1902. Surrey is a rich hunting ground for 'institution' architecture.

Farley Heath

The chief interest here lies in a comparison with neighbouring Shamley Green. The latter is larger and has been smartened up in typical county style whereas Farley is somehow rougher and more rural in an equally satisfying way. The grass is less trim and slopes attractively from the old farmhouse at the top. One side of the triangle has not been 'made up' yet and the dirt road helps to bring to life images from old photographs of these villages before they took on their present form.

The well-documented Romano-British settlement was centred on the heathland above the village. The road to Shamley Green passes to the left of the temple site which has been preserved with the foundations marked out. The road actually cuts through the site complex. (Not marked on all O.S. maps). Some of the discovered artifacts can be seen in Guildford Museum.

Here is a chance to see inside one of the traditional barns and view its roof timbers, because it has been converted into use as the local church. It is still black weather-boarded outside and stands at the edge of the farmyard. Inside it's plastered and lit by a little St Christopher window in the north wall. It also has an unusual early nineteenth century organ. All in all, well worth visiting.

Farncombe

'This almshouse was ye gifte of Richard Wyatt, Gent, citizen of London and Free of ye Company of ye Carpenters who died ye 8 of Novr: 1619.'

So says a brass plate showing Wyatt, his wife and six children. It can be seen in the chapel of the almshouses but he wasn't buried here. He lies at Isleworth. This was however, close to his country retreat of Hall Place at Shackleford. He also had land at Chiddingfold, Compton, Dunsfold and Hambledon which entitled the last three places to send one poor man each to the 'Oyspitall' with two from Puttenham and five from adjacent Goldalming. The buildings were ready for them in 1622 and a new quadrangle of cottages were added thirty years ago.

They are worth getting out of the traffic to see especially if you know Abbot's Hospital at the top of Guildford High Street. Both were completed in the same year and yet how they differ!

All of Farncombe seems to indicate post-railway development but walk up over the level crossing and there is some unexpected black and white half-timbering. There's more over the Godalming Navigation amidst the industrial archaeology of Catteshall. On the Navigation is Farncombe Boathouse from which boats can be hired to explore this extension of the Wey Navigation, added in 1760–2.

At Farncombe the railway station was built for Godalming in 1849 but that became a goods yard, primarily for paper from Catteshall Mill when the present Godalming station was opened further down the line in 1859. That left Farncombe needing a station, which was duly provided in 1897.

Fetcham

◄ The old mill pond out in the cornfield is now a nature reserve. The much-used public footpath beside it makes it somewhat disturbed but provides smooth access for wheelchairs. In spring and autumn it's a good place to spot migratory birds resting and feeding before continuing their journeys. In winter too it can attract less common species of gulls etc. as there are few stretches of open water for birds moving south of the London reservoirs.

Otherwise Fetcham is primarily a residential village with the usual few old buildings hiding among all the modern ones. The Norman arches in the church indicate its antiquity though. This is one of the few villages that was not plundered by William the Conqueror's men when they moved through Surrey after the Battle of Hastings. It belonged to Queen Edith, wife of Edward the Confessor and her Surrey lands were respected. This is one piece of evidence supporting the claim that Edward promised England to William.

In the later troubled times of 1625 Buckingham had a review of the County Horse on the Downs here as part of his war policy. That was on 28th November but it's always good to walk the Downs especially across to Norbury Park and down to the river again at Mickleham. There are plenty of hidden corners in that direction. More conspicuous is an oak tree in a field that is pointed out as having been planted to mark the centre of Surrey, but other parishes hotly dispute this!

Forest Green

How aptly this place is named. The Green is vast, carved out of the forest and still left superbly wild, all long grasses, flowers and butterflies. Along its fringes it still jostles with the forest. To the north the Leith Hill range rises abruptly and powerfully. Leith Hill Place, up there on the flanks, was the home of Dr. Ralph Vaughan Williams and through his family connections brings Charles Darwin and Josiah Wedgwood into the local history. The estate is now in the care of The National Trust, giving access to the wooded slopes with their massed displays of Rhododendrons and azaleas. (The house is not open to the public.) Entry can be made at the bend in the road at the north end of the Green. From up on the slopes there're impressive views over the Weald and also down onto Forest Green seen as a few rooftops in a clearing in a forest. How surprising to be able to make such an observation so close to London!

The masses of bluebells hereabouts are excellent biological indicators that these are indeed ancient woods. Some of the fields are still small enclosures just as when they were first 'assarted' from the woods hundreds of years ago. Some are still divided by narrow strips of woodland ('shaws') instead of hedges and still with the remains of their original banks and ditches.

Backwoods and backward; the remoteness lasted well into

this century. When Dr. Ralph Vaughan Williams was collecting folk music this was one of the places he visited and found that oral tradition surviving. From here was collected the song that became 'O Little Town of Bethlehem', sung for him by a labourer called Mr. Garman. 'Gosterwood' was named after its place of collection just to the south east of Forest Green.

Something worthwhile came to this village out of grief. Back in 1892 young Everard Hensley, aged eighteen, went hunting rabbits with his cousin who then unfortunately accidentally shot Everard. The hamlet had no church and so he was buried at Holmbury St. Mary but his parents decided to build a church here as a memorial to their son. It is a small, plain building, seating only ninety, down at the corner of the green nearest Ewhurst, but don't be put off. Step inside and you will find one of the most beautiful Victorian interiors in Surrey. Its beauty relies entirely on its unaffected simplicity and pleasing proportions. The east end is an embracing apse, tempting the eye to run around the fine woodwork of the roof, lit by three hanging lamps. The stained glass windows, memorials to the Hensley and related Burney families, include one to the luckless Everard.

Frensham

Gardeners all over the country will know this name as that of a rose. It was bred in Surrey in 1946 by crossing Crimson Glory with an un-named seedling. It has clusters of cheery red flowers and bright glossy leaves. Newer varieties are more disease-resistant, however, so Frensham is less often seen nowadays.

Others will think of the two ponds in the common which attract thousands of people every year. Back in 1913 the first seaplane was tested here.

For a little corner of old England though, take the turning through the village towards Dockenfield until you come to the Mill. You can't miss it for here the road swings in a great curve over the mill race frothing out into a great wide pool. It is an impressive piece of landscaping, so much more attractive than the usual sharp bends on to a straight causeway. The swallows loop and dip over the waters in summer and then zip up into the darkness of the sluices. The edges are rich in flowers: orange balsam and purple loosestrife, jagged spikes of gypsywort and pale blue twinkles of the water forget-me-not, the deadly hemlock and even the true bullrush if you can recognise it.

Beyond it the Wey meadows creep into Hampshire with Pitt Farm in the centre. You know it's nearly Hampshire for the shade of brick and tile is more yellow than the rosy tint so typical of most of Surrey. These farm roofs are also yellowed with lichen where they catch the damp westerlies blowing up the valley. In particular the roofs of the old oast houses catch the eye. Until recent times this was all great hop country through this corner of Surrey, joining with the hop fields of Hampshire serving the four breweries local to Alton.

It is a long tradition. Hops were first grown in the Farnham district in 1643 according to one authority. Then the plant was as controversial as is smoking 'pot' today. The hops go to the Hop Marketing Board nowadays rather than sustaining local industry. The decline has been hastened by a fall in demand, not because we drink less beer but because new strains of hop have been bred with a higher acid level so reducing the quantity required.

This is no longer a site for milling either but the imposing Mill House remains in red brick Georgian style, big and square and well maintained. It makes a very satisfying focal point in the scene. There's a footpath between it and the outbuilding which leads up along the river. Watch for kingfishers.

Eventually you will come to a long pool, very popular with birds for it is quieter and more wooded here than around the Great Pond which lies a little further up. The path emerges at the Great Pond beside the dam itself, right on the

Hampshire border. Below and against the dam on the downstream side notice a hollow, now rather overhung with bushes. This was the local sheep dip.

A dam was built here at least as early as Norman times to create a fish pond for the Church; some say for the Bishop of Winchester, some say for the monks of Waverley Abbey. The fish were reared in small 'stew ponds' and remnants of these have now been incorporated into the hotel garden by the dam. You can't miss them but you might not recognise them for what they are.

The original boggy pool has long since been extended into a great sheet of water stretching away to the heathland barrier of the King's Ridge. Here Bronze Age people buried their dead under 'bowl barrows'. Below the ridge on the other side lies the Little Pond, also medieval, and not so little.

If you can, come very early in the morning when it's just you and the ponds and the season and the birds. See the swans coming in to land, forcing their wing-tips down onto the ice to break their speed before daring to put their feet down. Later in the year, catch the newly-hatched coots when they have still got their astonishing orange heads. Watch the thin autumn sun shift the mist over the water to reveal rafts of ducks that have dropped in for the night and look for rarities. Many a rare moment has been caught here; great grey shrikes out on the common, the great reed warbler at the water's edge, the occasional osprey even, dropping in for a quick fish on its migratory journey to Africa.

For different scenes, try a walk through the little district of Shortfield Common where its common is not heather and gorse but long green grass falling down the sandy hillside amid the trees.

Friday Street

➤ 'There's not much here' my companion commented; and that's its glory. No pavements, no yellow lines, no street furniture, no commercial buildings except a pub. There aren't even any cars; they have to be left outside the hamlet. All you'll find, in a hollow in the woods, is a fine wide pool and a few Surrey-style homes of brick and stone and tile. It's beautiful but don't all pour in to see it or you will spoil its tranquillity!

Gatton

➤ Colman's Mustard is well enough known but he has given us more than that. In 1952 over a hundred acres of his woodlands were given to The National Trust. Apart from mustard the plant associated with the name of Sir Jeremiah Colman was the orchid and at Gatton he raised his own hybrids. He also chaired the Orchid Committee of The Royal Horticultural Society.

Over a hundred acres of the parkland at Gatton have been acquired by The National Trust so much of this place should remain safe from building development. There's no real village at Gatton – it was one of the most notorious of the 'Rotten Boroughs'.

The church, in the Park (access permitted) is packed with unusual interest brought together last century by Lord Monson from various parts of Europe. The woodwork is particularly impressive, with the nave seated longways with Baroque stalls from Ghent. There's panelling from Aarschot Cathedral in Brabant and more from Burgundy. The doors came from Rouen. The altar rails came from Tongres in Belgium. The list goes on and on. As much comes from the sixteenth century it's a rare opportunity to compare the varying continental styles and relate them to our own.

Gomshall

➤ Alas much of Gomshall is strung along the busy A25 and so closely fills its space that little is left for car parking. The Tillingbourne runs beside the road and beside the river runs the famous tannery. Gomshall has been a centre for tanning since at least the 16th century and several of the old buildings have been so connected in the past.

One building, after several name changes, is called King John House and is a splendid brick building of c.1620, where Queen Street leaves the main road. It conceals an older house behind. It is thus unlikely to have been built from the proceeds of hides collected after the London plague of 1666, as local tradition would have us believe. It has been a tannery though.

Further up Queen Street a black and white half-timbered wing calls attention to an old farmhouse which also served as a tannery at one time. The adjoining cottages (Nos 1–8), although not centuries old, are worth a second glance for the subtle patterning of stone-laying in the ground floors. It's not typical of Surrey. The use of tiles, with patterns in those too, helps maintain the continuity of local building practice.

Tanning is an interesting industry for Surrey because it was banned in all areas where William the Conqueror and his successors imposed Forest Law. William tried to do that over all Surrey to maintain good and convenient hunting grounds but he did not succeed in taking the whole of the county. Soon certain districts won exemption although others had to wait over six hundred years to gain freedom. Gomshall was fortunate in this respect and had the additional asset of sufficient good water from the Tillingbourne. Under Forest Law (as opposed to Common Law) tanning was banned in case it encouraged poaching of the King's deer.

Otherwise this was an agricultural village like everywhere else. There is a reminder of this with the *Black Horse* pub. Black Horses was an earlier name for the breed of carthorse that we now call Shire Horses – those beautiful animals that ploughed the pattern into Surrey's countryside once they'd superseded oxen as draught animals.

Nearby is the United Reformed Church. It's an early chapel of 1821 that had to be enlarged in 1887. It is plain, of red brick, with broad lancet windows divided by Y-tracery – the sort described as 'Churchwarden windows'.

Grafham

Imagine a tall distinguished gentleman of forty eight, dressed as per usual in a loose blue serge suit with a crimson silk tie. This is the eminent Victorian architect, Henry Woodyer, inspecting the final stages in the building of Grafham church (1864). The light catches the small steel brooch in his wide brimmed black hat as he passes inside; a hint of self-assertion about his slightly informal appearance. This was to be his own church from his own personal funds and he was having it the way he liked it. The Bishop of Winchester did not like screens but Woodyer did and was definitely going to have one. So he built it of stone, integral with the main fabric and there was nothing the bishop could do about it. With a swish of his Inverness cloak he returns to Grafham Grange, the home he designed for himself across the road, leaving just a whiff from one of his highly scented cigars.

Great Bookham

One of the great love stories of Surrey is between the eighteenth century novelist Fanny Burney and General Alexandre d'Arblay seeking refuge in Juniper Hall, Mickleham after fleeing the French Revolution. Fanny had already fallen foul of censure for resigning her position at the royal court as Second Keeper of the Robes. Now she incurred more, especially from her father, when her attention was caught by the aristocratic, but unfortunately foreign, soldier. He had been second in command under Lafayette. Fanny, at forty one, had a mind of her own and soon a husband too. They were married on July 31st 1793 in Mickleham church and moved to Great Bookham in the November. They chose Fairfield, a small red brick house with garden and orchard, which still stands in the High Street. (It has been heightened and enlarged since then). Here they settled down to a very happy period in their lives. Fanny set about writing *Camilla*. This the General 'corrected' for her but as he was still having lessons in English for six hours a day he didn't make too good a job of it! In December 1795 a son was born to them. The following April he was christened Alexander Charles Louis Piochard in the parish church of Great Bookham by the Rev. Samuel Cooke.

By June *Camilla* was finished, all 1370 pages of it in five volumes. Subscriptions were collected to help guarantee its success but the publishers were so confident they paid the highest ever copyright fee – £1,000. They were right. It became the fastest selling Guinea Book. With the proceeds the d'Arblays moved out of Great Bookham to West Humble (hence Camilla Lacey) beyond Norbury Park where their friends lived. It's probably the basis for Fanny's *Beech Park*.

That's not quite the end of the story for Great Bookham. The Rev. Samuel Cooke had a teenage god-daughter called Jane Austen whose name appears on the subscription list for *Camilla*. It's not known whether Fanny ever met young Jane, as the first recorded visit of Jane to Bookham was not until 1809. What is more certain is that Jane did read her copy of *Camilla* and took her own title *Pride and Prejudice* from the last paragraph where Fanny used it three times in block capitals.

The Rectory where she would have stayed was demolished in 1961. It was behind the shops in Church Road but the cedar tree survives. Much of the surrounding landscape was used by Jane Austen including the famous sequence of the picnic on Box Hill from *Emma*.

Hale

➤ 'What a terrifying place this is! It must be the House of God; it must be the gate that opens into Heaven.' So reads part of Genesis 28, verse 17 and from this came the Hebrew 'Bethel' for House of God. In the nineteenth century the Non-Conformists took this word for their chapels. At Hale they built such a chapel as early as 1834 on a spot long used for outdoor preaching. The date is quite significant in the Baptist revival movement. In that year the doctrine was re-introduced into Europe and the first chapel opened in Hamburg.

Hale's chapel is reached up Bethel Lane, an attractive little backwater after all the jagged traffic and some rather jarring housing estates around the village. It's high above Farnham looking widely over the Wey Vale to the Hindhead Hills. Even here there are reminders of the hopfields of earlier days including White Bine Cottages below the chapel. They date from 1888 but are quite plain compared with their contemporaries further north in Surrey. The only relief comes from the rhomboid white lintels. Otherwise they are plain brick but that lovely orange brick peculiar to this district. Plain red brick was good enough for Elm Cottages (1893) a little further up.

Thus we can see the settlement growing around the chapel. That in itself is quite a surprise. It is a low cuboid, quite domestic, with soft coloured rendering and rectangular windows. It's not the usual non-conformist architecture at all, not big and bold and out of keeping with its neighbours. In fact, it's not terrifying at all!

Hambledon

➤ With so many old timbered cottages to enjoy from the outside it is especially rewarding to be able to come here and see the inside of one (by arrangement). Oakhurst Cottage is owned by The National Trust but is too tiny and without suitable parking to be opened to the public in the normal way. Inside it is still remarkably traditional and houses part of the Gertrude Jekyll Collection of West Surrey bygones for added authenticity. The local National Trust leaflet gives details for arranging a visit.

The National Trust also own the little green that makes a delightful nook up the narrow lane to the church and Court Farm. The latter is very attractive with its tile hanging, as is its granary nearby. Both are listed and the whole group forms a conservation area. Another National Trust house, not open to the public at all, is Glebe House of 1710. It's different from the usual Surrey style; five bays of stone with brick dressings but still gabled.

Later still, 1786, is the Union Workhouse, now converted for government use but preserving what was worthwhile.

Hambledon was the home of Eric Parker who wrote about Surrey so well for some fifty years, beginning with his *Highways and Byeways in Surrey* in 1908. Other subjects came into his writings and he was editor of *The Field* too.

Hascombe

◄ High in the hills with beautiful scenery and walks all around this small village is still remote. How much more so it must have been by horse in medieval times, yet here lived Nicholas Hussey, Sheriff of Surrey and Sussex. He served Henry VI and continued into the reign of Edward IV who soon charged Nicholas with not having paid his dues since he'd come to the throne. The problem was sorted out and Nicholas was pardoned in 1467.

As a younger son he was lucky to be doing so well anyway. That good fortune arose from his elder brother being outlawed and having to forfeit his rights. The site of the Hussey homestead is believed to be that of Hascombe

Place, not open to the public, but visible from the footpath that leads up into the woods and hills from beside the village pub.

Another lane from this spot leads to the village pond, one of a chain of ancient fish ponds. It's always a good place for birds especially with its little island in the middle. Here the dabchick can be regularly seen, with greater ease than elsewhere. Nearby stands the church, rebuilt in 1864 by the important architect, Henry Woodyer and it is one of his finest works. It's rather High Church but that suited the rector, Vernon Musgrave. It was part of his programme to pull Hascombe up by its bootlaces. He did too, and became a familiar figure with his shaggy beard and dog to match.

At the northern end of the village is Winkworth Arboretum, once the private collection of Dr. Wilfrid Fox who planted closely for autumn colour rather than for specimen trees. He intended it for the National Trust after his death – rarely does the Trust have a property made specially for it! Look out for a *Sorbus* called 'Wilfrid Fox' named after him and an *Acer* called 'Madeline Spitta' named after his secretary.

There are top and bottom entrances so the disabled can enjoy much of the collection despite it being over a steep hillside. The autumn colours from beside the lake are recommended.

Headley

◣ Step into the churchyard and you are confronted by a most peculiar building. It's a rough stone dome with an open front, sheltering a Victorian font, of all things. Behind it, in the wall is a medieval window, now blocked. Around the walls are slate panels, once bearing, more clearly, the Ten Commandments. To see all this closely you have to step round a memorial slab to Elizabeth and Ferdinand Faithful, for this is their family's vault, made from the remains of the old church on the site. The exact position of the church is marked in the churchyard behind by a row of clipped yews.

To the north was built the new church with the tower and spire that have become such a well known local landmark. It's all Victorian. The Surrey-style chamfered edge was not given to the spire so it remains square in section from top to bottom. More interesting are the church walls. They're of flint but show, all in one view, the different effects that can be achieved.

The nave wall is built from whole flints but instead of them being the usual grey they are a warm russet colour. Although laid in rather strict courses they protrude far enough for side lighting to cast bold shadows to enrich the visual as well as the tactile texture of the wall. The chancel wall is of knapped flints with the split surfaces creating the wall's face. Again, these are stained russet right through, giving a wonderful colour and pattern to the wall. It's most unusual for Surrey. The tower walls are in complete contrast, being of knapped flint again but in the usual black and grey. What a hard appearance it has!

The nave and chancel were built from locally gathered flints while the tower was built with those salvaged from the old church. Two different architects worked at the job. The knapped flint work of both chancel and tower was guided by George Edmund Street (see Holmbury St. Mary). The nave is by Anthony Salvin who was more at ease with secular architecture, especially castles, and restored both Windsor and the Tower of London.

There is a sundial over the south door; one especially designed for a wall but it is not set flush with the wall because the wall doesn't in fact face due south. The inscription on it can be difficult to read in some lights but is 'Nil nisi coelestre radio' (I am nothing without light from above.) Old sundials are a great rarity in Surrey churchyards.

The high airy places about Headley attract many walkers but its remoteness has also ensured that parts are still worth preserving for their ecological value. Parts of the Heath are now a nature reserve and so is Nower Wood – a scarce example of 'ancient' woodland. Access is regularly offered by the Surrey Wildlife Trust.

Hindhead

'Replace lid firmly to keep contents airtight.' How often we've read something like that on the instructions on food containers. Here lived the man who discovered the connection between decay and air-borne germs. He was Professor John Tyndall who began life as an Irish railway engineer. He took the Victorian education ideals to heart, set off on a life's self-improvement course and won the patronage of Michael Faraday whom he eventually succeeded. Light, sound, heat; they all came under his scrutiny but he loved the natural world too, from the majesty of glaciers to the humble heather and gorse of the local commons. These he expressly wished to be planted on his grave (his wife accidentally gave him an overdose of medicine) which is in the cemetery opposite Haslemere church. He didn't want a headstone; he gave his money away for scholarships. He would never have guessed what his lasting memorial would be. He claimed that the air at Hindhead was so pure and so enriched with pine essence that it was as good as that in Switzerland. Consequently people saved their Swiss health cure money to build villas about the Hindhead Hills, conveniently served by the new railway. The lichens show the air to be as polluted now as elsewhere in Surrey!

They are still building but his own home has been developed into flats with a Close, 'Tyndalls' of course. It's just south of the traffic lights. Opposite, there are walks into the pine trees, down through acres of preserved woodland into a quiet secluded valley. Such valleys are called 'bottoms' hereabouts.

Alternatively, behind Tyndalls, there are numerous walks over the heather and gorse of Hindhead Common. There are fine views all around with Gibbet Hill, the most famous of all, ahead. Apart from the Old Portsmouth Coaching Road that is well known there are other stretches of coach road visible out on the Common that once linked it with Haslemere.

Tea can be taken back in Hindhead at the *Undershaw Hotel*, once the home of Sir Arthur Conan Doyle, of Sherlock Holmes fame. Another house he used is further down Hindhead Road but not visible.

Holmbury St. Mary

The elements of local style are rapidly and indelibly registered when touring Surrey villages and it's so easy to forget that it is comparatively new. Most of the cosy red brick cottages with tile hung walls and white paintwork date only from Victorian times. They fit so well, so often, because the Victorians had a good sense of scale and of place. Nowhere, on a small scale, can that be better appreciated than by standing on the church steps at Holmbury St. Mary and looking down the very steep hillside on to the tiny triangular green with the cottages nestling around. It all looks just right yet much is only nineteenth century.

The church was built in 1879 by G. E. Street, the architect already famous for London's Law Courts etc. He, and especially his wife, fell in love with Holmbury St. Mary and built 'Holmdale' to move to, although Mrs Street died too soon. He built the church at his own expense and it is one of his most notable. Best of all is that the developments they initiated haven't spoilt the place.

Looking up at the church from the green, it doesn't look anything very special at all. That's what is special about it. It says more about the architect's respect for local style and place and less about his own self-importance. Inside, however, a building creates its own setting and here we come closer to the great man and the Oxford Movement.

It has a certain richness from its blue Pennant stone columns with marble shafts and tiled patterned flooring but they do not overpower. The walls of local stone and the space itself keep all in harmony. Nothing is specifically noticeable; all has to be noticed. The glint from brass candelabra, the sparkle of stained glass, flat images from paintings, shadows incised into sculpture, the eye finds them all and they all reward. It's the best of its type in Surrey.

Hooley

A horse-drawn tramway on iron rails was built into Surrey in 1802 from Wandsworth. It was given the imposing title of the Grand Surrey Iron Railway and was the first such thing to be publicly owned. In 1810 it was extended all the way to Blechingley for the chalk and fullers earth from Nutfield and Merstham.

Those keen on industrial archaeology will find preserved at Hooley a bridge and a section of earthworks belonging to the former railway. In 1951 the County Council re-erected a portion of the track by *The Joliffe Arms* on London Road North at Merstham.

Horne

The village school is remarkable, not for its architecture but for its date – 1910. Most villages had made such provision long before then. It's still rather a remote and little-known village, mostly farms. There are a couple of good traditional groups that can be viewed from the lanes, one still with a granary on staddle stones.

Really it is only the church that asserts there is a village at all. It was restored in 1880 by G. M. Hills who has been much condemned for it. Maybe he did destroy practically all of the old one but at least he left a pleasing decent building of traditional materials used in a traditional way. Thus it looks very much a rural church and has a village atmosphere inside.

Thankfully some of the old fittings were kept – the font, chest, screen and a Jacobean monument, in particular. The last is one with kneeling figures that's so boringly repetitive but this one is special. It still has its original colouring, soft and faded but still very effective. Opposite, behind the curtain, is the explanation for the intriguing little pierced quarterfoil noticeable in the outside wall. It's a tiny window. It lights a flight of stone stairs that go up inside the thickness of the medieval wall, to provide access to the pre-Reformation rood loft. Although they are not rare in England as a whole, they are rare in this county.

Horsell

Horsell is known to booklovers near and far as being the place chosen by H. G. Wells for the landing of the Martians in *The War of the Worlds*. The sand pit that inspired his landing site still exists out on the common, and was cleared of tree seedlings in 1986. Wells wrote the book while living near Woking station (1895–6) and it contains much accurate detail of the countryside surrounding the infant Woking. There were clear views across the heathlands to Horsell but now trees blot it out. Woking has grown and belly-flopped over the heaths. The scattering of old Horsell cottages still lie embedded in the later development like pips in a tomato sandwich.

Horsell was one of the villages to develop more fully during the late twelfth century expansion and parts of the parish church survive from that time, although most of what we see is from the later Middle Ages. It is there to see though. Some references make it sound entirely Victorian, which a lot of it is. But the church as a whole is not as depressing as some books lead us to believe.

One thing to note that always seems to have escaped notice, even in the new church guide is that part of the 'handsome Gothic Screen' was retained in 1840. The present screen incorporates the cusped heads of its medieval predecessor in the two northern bays. Run your fingers over the woodwork and you can feel the difference. You will also note that on the west side it was more richly carved and this has been planed off. The southernmost bay has been carved to match.

There is documentary proof that the pulpit was provided in 1602, so Horsell was to the fore in those days for they were not compulsory furnishings until 1603. It is still more Elizabethan than Jacobean in its detailing. Don't miss the doors under the tower either. They are fine medieval workmanship with their original ironwork too. For ironwork Horsell has the oddest of items. It's a 'brochis' or spit, for roasting meat at parish festivals, and that's old too, recorded in an inventory of 1552. Horsell church has much more of interest – it hasn't all been vandalised. The Suttons feared this. In 1603 their memorials were inscribed 'Gentle reader deface not this stone'.

Hurst Green

'Inept' says Ian Nairn's *Buildings of England* referring to the parish church here. That must surely be worth seeing. It took some finding too, in a suburban backwater; easy only when you know how.

Like its suburban surroundings the churchyard was smartly mown (no headstones), the roses duly pruned and flowering colourfully, the conifers wired into regular shapes. Whatever other people think of it, the church was obviously well cared for by the community it served. It looked every bit its 1912 date with blank flint walls of stark regularity; quoins and tracery equally intent upon their purpose. Still in the Gothic Revival phase this pseudo-

Decorated building doesn't capture the spirit of its medieval model. It looks like a job from the drawing board, not from the heart.

Walk round to the west end though and you find a small rose window that isn't imitation but a genuine thought from its own age. See it when the sun is in the west and have the red and blue glass throw strange purples and violets over your face as you view it from inside. They are very bright, very transparent colours, taking little from their Victorian forerunners. It is emblematic rather than representational, with a striking cockerel (for St. Peter) in the lower portion.

Before leaving there is one little quirk to smile upon. Over the north arcade there are carvings, just as there would be in a 14th century church, including the modern counterpart of the master mason's head. It is well carved, cloth cap and all, even with his initials below.

The design may be inept but the church has a dash of colour and gives you a smile.

The Green is a marvellous airy space flung over the top of a hill like a cloth for a picnic and sitting in the countryside around are some of the county's best old farmhouses. You come across these unexpectedly in the lanes over the clay lands below the ridges.

Hydestile

➤ Where the lands beyond Milford run up to the Hascombe hills and Winkworth Arboretum is the district of Hydestile. There's no village as such, just scattered homes and a group of hospitals, to which St. Thomas's was evacuated during the Second World War and stayed long after.

The crest of the hill is Hydon Ball, a national memorial to Octavia Hill, co-founder of The National Trust. Below is Hydon Nursery. Here Mr. A. George has been very successfully breeding new rhododendrons. Seeking a version that would remain small to suit modern gardens he chose for the main parent the beautiful pink rhododendron yakushi-manum. They by patiently cross-fertilizing by hand and nurturing the seedlings to the flowering stage he has been able to select and perpetuate a valuable new series. Most of these are pre-fixed 'Hydon' of which 'Hydon Dawn' has been the most popular.

Species of rhododendron new to cultivation often begin life in Britain at this nursery too. Such is his skill that when fresh seed is collected during a plant collection expedition in some remote corner of the globe, it will eventually arrive here to be germinated and nurtured along with the love and care that only such a skilled enthusiast can give.

Kingswood Warren

➤ The local Vansittart family, in the nineteenth century, moved to Shottesbrooke Park in Berkshire where they were of course visited by their friends. One of these was the lord of the manor, Lieutenant Colonel Thomas Alcock who was so taken with the church that had been built in the Park in 1337 that he had a replica built on his land back home at Kingswood. He laid the first stone himself on 13th April 1848 and was also present for its consecration on 23rd September 1852.

The architect to whom he entrusted this task was Benjamin Ferrey – not a name to raise our expectations very high but here he excelled himself. He must surely have enjoyed the work because he has brought the 'soul' of the church to Surrey as well as the measurements. It shows how insensitive so many of the Victorian architects could be (including himself on occasions alas!). Compare this with Brockham which he'd only just finished.

Four years later Alcock died, in his ninety fourth year and his memorial on the north chancel wall gives us a fuller picture of this dear old eccentric. In 1780 he'd joined the Honourable East India Company, serving in Bengal successively as Military Secretary, Deputy Adjutant General and then Quartermaster General of the Army in the Field before returning to England to serve for eight years as Treasurer of the Ordnance. His friends, the Vansittarts, can be met again in the history of Ewell where Henrietta continued the work of her father, James Lowe, and patented the Lowe-Vansittart Propellor.

Kingswood church is hidden in the trees beside the A217 and can only be reached from the southbound carriageway (roundabouts nearby for correcting errors!).

Laleham

◣ Right up under the eaves of a two-storey house on the main road can be spotted a fine sundial. Dated 1730 it gives added distinction to Dial House which is also early eighteenth century. Possibly the first owners added it. There's more richly coloured brickwork in the old cottage next door.

There is much to please the explorer so don't be put off by the traffic and modern development. Take one of the quiet lanes down to the Thames. You'd hardly know the river was there. Try Blacksmith Lane opposite the church for example, which soon leaves the classical town architecture behind and slips into the vernacular. There's Old Barn Cottage for example, nothing madly exciting but when the county has so many half-timbered barn conversions it's of added interest to see their all-brick counterparts in the Thames Valley. Forge Cottage is simple but smart, and shows the local habit of whitening the bricks.

Where the lane opens on to the river bank there's an old weathered stone either side, at the foot of the walls. Just discernible are the Arms of the City of London – old boundary stones. Turn left and the open spaces of Laleham Park are reached but only because they were snatched back from developers in 1931. They'd managed to build only three of their proposed three hundred houses. Instead £300 was spent on trees and the Park was handed over for public use.

The next year the Park house was bought by the Community of St. Peter the Apostle for seventy-nine sisters and a

Mother Superior. Probably this is the site of a much earlier monastic foundation for Edward the Confessor gave the manor to Westminster Abbey and a grange was established. Granges were outlying farms administered by the monks, especially the Cistercians, although Westminster was Benedictine. By the end of the Middle Ages they were often used as country retreats for all manner of purposes.

The history of the site becomes more interesting in 1803 when tradition says the Government bought the estate at auction and then swopped it with the second Earl of Lucan for his Irish estates. The Earl promptly brought in the Prince Regent's architect, John Buonarotti Papworth, who pushed fashion forwards with his advanced new house. Today we can peep through the gates and still be impressed by the bold Greek Doric, diminishing in scale as the eye rises to the swan weather vane twirling in the wind.

The Earl's son commanded the cavalry at Balaclava. His brother-in-law, Lord Cardigan, led the Charge of the Light Brigade. The fourth Earl entertained Edward VII here until his debts finished his life in High Society. Previously there had been another royal visitor, Queen Maria of Portugal, from 1829 to 1834 when she was still in her minority. It is said that her bedroom was so large that it was later divided into five!

In complete contrast, the nearby Thatched Cottage has also been attributed to Papworth. It's a delightful example of the 'cottage orne' style of which Surrey has so few examples. It offers so much to please the eye, from its tall yellow chimney pots down to its sweeps of thatch, and verandah supported on rustic wooden poles; from its intricately glazed windows to bright yellow and highly decorative bargeboards.

Further along Abbey Drive the eye is caught by The Coverts, about a century older, dating from about 1700. Next to notice, but not noticeable, is Muncaster House. This was purchased in 1819 by the Rev. John Buckland and his brother-in-law, the Rev. Thomas Arnold. The former started the country's first preparatory school and it flourished here until 1911. Buckland retired in 1853 and was succeeded by his son, the Rev. Matthew Harvey Buckland and he in turn, in 1883, by Francis Buckland who moved the school to Bexhill to escape the Thames damp. He died in 1913 but is buried at Laleham.

As for that Thomas Arnold, he worked with the older children preparing them for university, until he moved on to become the famous headmaster of Rugby School. His family connection with Laleham lasted over a century and their gravestones are to be found in the churchyard, south of the chancel. His house was demolished in 1864 and the bricks used to build the school on the adjoining plot. It still stands and the old bricks are readily discernible. The Glebe House to the left marks the site of the Arnolds' house. Together with School Cottage to the right, of 1873 with the Lucan coat of arms, they all make a good nineteenth century corner in The Broadway.

Further along, Nos.35–39 of 1876 make a good comparison. The broad gabled block is simple and dignified, in yellow brick rather than red, except for red lintels and their bonding course. The roof had restrained decorative tiling, part of which remains. The Glebe House (built as the rectory) was highly decorated compared with contemporary buildings in this neighbourhood. It must have been quite a trend-setter in its day.

Back by the church is Church Farm, dating back to at least the early seventeenth century and having housed several famous visitors, including Bob Hope in 1961. Round the corner is Shepperton Road where No.4 was rented by Gertrude Lawrence for several years. *The Three Horseshoes* had William Clifton as licensee for over forty years up to 1925 and he hosted the Prince of Wales. Sir Arthur Sullivan acted as barman one Easter Monday. There are tales all about Laleham, even on the headstones:-

> As long as life both day and night
> My time with care did spend
> My bread to get through cold
> In pain my days did end.   (1748)

or more cheerfully:-

> Why do ye mourn departed friends
> Or shake at death's alarms?
> 'Tis but the voice that Jesus sends
> To call me to his arms   (1842)

Leigh

The name is pronounced nowadays to rhyme with sky but was formerly pronounced 'Lee' because in 1499 Richard Arderne requested in his will that he be buried before the image of St. Katherine at the church at 'the Lee'. He was too. There's still the indent for the memorial brass to him and his wife Joan. They had no children. Alas these effigies are now lost although the supporting brass scrolls, inscription and heraldic shields remain.

Nearby is the brass effigy to his aunt Susanna and his paternal grandparents. They represented an important but not unfamiliar story for Surrey. The proximity of the county to London fostered the practice of having a town house for business and a country retreat. This had always been the case with the nobility who ranged from one estate to another but by the later Middle Ages the newly rising middle classes could afford two properties. Such was the case with Richard Arderne who rose to be sheriff of Surrey and Sussex in 1432. He had his town house in Whitefriars and his country house at Leigh, just as some people today have a holiday villa in Spain as their second property.

The Ardernes did well. Look at all the fur with which they are represented. It edges his gown and lines his mantle and hood. His wife's mantle is fur-lined too. Their six children are shown with them. The images of the three daughters are of note for their unusual hair styles. Each is shown with her hair being worn with side cauls beneath a simple band. One of these little girls is Susanna whose own memorial brass lies nearby. Notice that much of the image is the same as that on their parents' brass. The lettering is very similar too. It has been suggested that both brasses came from the same workshop at the same time, probably on the death of the mother and before that of the father as there is no inscription and one was never added.

Leaving them behind we step out of the church into the green and spreading Vale of Holmsdale. They chose a good place to live. The Priest's House to the south is said to have been the lodging, until the Dissolution of the Monasteries, of the visiting priest supplied by Newark Priory. This arrangement was evidently cheaper than funding a resident priest. Out along Clayhill Road is Clayhill Farm which I am told was a convalescent home for nuns – hence its church-like appearance.

Limpsfield

Delius the composer was buried here in 1934 followed by his wife eleven months later. Despite the pilgrims it attracts it is difficult to find their grave because the churchyard is so big and has an extraordinary number of headstones. Soem are old with beautiful lettering and extended inscriptions to catch the eye. The Delius one is not conspicuous but sits comfortably among its neighbours on the north side between the church and the yew tree. The inscription can be read from the seat under the yew. There's quite a variety of trees here, including a fine *Catalpa*. Masses of perky harebells hug the headstones where the deadly mower can't reach and purple toadflax spires up out of the boundary wall.

You're really conscious of stone here. The paths are composed of smooth purplish ironstone sets. Rough dark lumps of ironstone create the church walls, with the rich brown local sandstone. There are even chunky slabs of stone for the roof ('Horsham slates'). The spire of oak shingles, leaning a

bit to the west is square from top to bottom and so doesn't have the more usual Surrey-style chamfered edge.

The starkly whitened interior is sadly disappointing. But on leaving, notice the lychgate. No one else seems to, yet it is original, dating from 1350 and possibly the only such survivor in Surrey. It looks ordinary because the Victorians mass-produced the idea but squared it up. The design here is long and narrow, stretching its old timbers across the path in two stages under one heavy roof of Horsham slabs. 'Lych' comes from the Saxon for corpse, for here in former days the corpse was rested for the burial service, instead of in church as we might expect today. At Chiddingfold the 'table' for the coffin remains under the lychgate.

Beyond can be seen the village street climbing up to the main road. Everything sits comfortably here too. Modern infilling is not too obtrusive and there's a strong impression of love and care. It must always have been so judging from the number of fine old buildings which have survived. The Court Cottage group is well known and so is Detellins further up. The latter is open to the public at certain times and is worth seeing as one of the most interesting fifteenth century houses in the county. It is a medieval hall-house which had the typical central fireplace, entrance, screens etc. with wings at either end. In the eighteenth century it was drastically altered, hence the fine brick facade towards the street but much of the original house remains. There are many others worth a look especially for anyone who can read the building history from the visible evidence.

Limpsfield Chart

Limpsfield Chart, or The Chart, is a wild and windy place over the brow of the hill from Limpsfield. The National Trust and the Forestry Commission maintain large areas of woodland and common, popular for walking and wildlife but historic too. Step into certain areas and all around is the evidence of ancient woodland crafts such as coppicing, and rings of trees ever growing outwards from original coppice stools from the time when Limpsfield was just beginning.

There are some old houses worth finding but seek *The Grasshopper* pub. It's off the hill, down beside the main A25 so it is far from hidden. But its truth is! This is no ordinary pub but an enormous building that bounces in gables down to the car park and it's all half-timbered like a Tudor mansion. Its shape and proportions instantly tell it's not Tudor yet much of the timbering is weathered and obviously old. Indeed it is, having been lovingly collected from sites near and far and brought to create this strange folly in 1950.

Lingfield

Here you can find a little Turk lying on his side, with his bearded head wrapped in a turban and little brown feet popped into his sandals. So this was one of the dreaded Saracens whom we fought in the Holy Land to obtain safe access to Jerusalem. How astonishing he must have been to any fourteenth century folk admitted to the chancel of Lingfield's church. He supports the feet of the tomb effigy of an English knight, Reginald, the first Lord Cobham. (Kent's Cobham, not Surrey's).

It was he who, in 1431, founded a secular college here and rebuilt most of the church. In so doing he gave Surrey its most complete example of Perpendicular church architecture. Although it looks big from outside it in no way prepares you for the great impression of space that you find inside.

It houses much of interest including Surrey's only medieval choir stalls. Lift one of the seats (very carefully, the hinges are coming off) and you'll find a bracket supported by some very fine carving. This is a misericord or 'pity seat' to support those tiring of standing through the very long services. It is a pity it's called a seat as it is not for sitting on.

Stand in a stall and you'll find the armrests are just the height for taking the strain off the legs. Sag a little and the misericord supports your behind. Sag too much and down it swings, dumping you ingloriously on the floor, right in the middle of the service! But don't try this with one of the damaged seats. Explore the carvings instead. Some of it is of top national standard.

Outside there's no trace of the college but leave the churchyard by the north exit and there's a medieval timber-framed building tucked into the hillside. It was originally the guest house of the college.

It is possible to see the internal structure of one of these buildings as it now houses the County Library. Peer through the trees and see the recessed front with curved braces supporting the roof at this place. That's a wealden feature found more often in Kent than Surrey.

In the north churchyard spot the cherubs carved on some of the headstones. They are not common in Surrey either. A couple of nearby headstones have their tops chamfered back; most peculiar.

Back at the south entrance you get another set of exciting views of the old buildings forming a little square: soft weathered brickwork and lumbering timber work. The finest is a 15th century hall house with a 16th century wing projecting to the side of the square. Look again and you'll find an original shop window (now blocked); decidedly rare.

In my eyes at least this is the most beautiful architectural corner in Surrey.

Back in the main part of the village where the traffic streams through to the races there are a few other items to see. A weird stone building under an ancient oak tree, right on the roadside, will catch the eye. The tower part is a much restored medieval cross (c.1473) erected to designate the boundary between Billeshurst and Puttenden Manors. On to it, in 1773, was added a little prison, last used in 1882 to detain poachers.

Beside this is the village pond which was 'gardenised' for

Medieval miserichords.

the 1977 Royal Silver Jubilee but is a most attractive spot for an ice cream in summer. Note the greater spearwort growing there: our largest buttercup and not common in Surrey.

Full marks to the planners who have been more successful than elsewhere at ensuring modern infilling has not been too obtrusive. Note also, all the Victorian villas looking solid and sound yet unpretentious. No marks for guessing the railway had arrived!

Little Bookham

━━ You can quite easily drive through here without knowing it. Turn down Little Bookham Street though and you'll find ribbon development of the most attractive kind, reaching back to the sixteenth century, set back behind grassy verges, thankfully protected by the National Trust.

It's also worth turning up Manor House Lane to find the hidden church (up a gravelled drive off the sharp bend). Just for once you can see a church that has shrunk rather than developed over the centuries. Even when it's locked you can still see the arches and capitals of a blocked 12th century arcade on the south side where a former aisle has vanished. Tradition has it that the aisle was destroyed by fire during the thirteenth century. In 1986 the parish celebrated its nine hundredth anniversary and the lack of dedication, lost in time, was corrected with a new dedication service to 'All Saints'.

Littleton (near Spelthorne)

━━ The entwined initials 'RB' glow from a terracotta roundel on the gable end of a main road cottage. Presumably they mark an estate cottage from when the Burbridge family held Littleton Park (now Shepperton Film Studios). The Burbridge family vault can be found in the adjacent churchyard. It's one of those broken column types on a great masonry platform.

The church houses much of interest but even when locked its prime importance can still be viewed. It's the brickwork. Most counties have a tower or aisle from the seventeenth or eighteenth centuries but few can show sixteenth century work, as here. There are lovely Tudor windows on the south side, reminders of the superb Tudor brickwork at nearby Hampton Court Palace. Oddly, the influence of the Palace upon local architecture is slight. When Littleton was in Middlesex it was the only example of note. Now that it is in Surrey it still hasn't a rival. It's not all Tudor. Differences in the brickwork indicate the presence of later work. For example the top of the tower is later. The south porch is eighteenth century too. Inside it are the original bench seats, polished smooth after two centuries of people sitting.

There's not much else to see in this hamlet cowering under the massive ramparts of the reservoir. They need to be massive: the Queen Mary Reservoir is so big that waves of damaging size were whipped up on it and a barrier to break them was built. The calm waters behind the barrier were reserved as a bird sanctuary and a successful one at that. In the winter, particularly, a wide range of waterfowl may be driven south to here by bad weather. Thus southern watchers can tick off several species they wouldn't otherwise expect to see. Avoid windy days; the bitter blast off the water into your face makes for a memorable watch!

Littleton (near Guildford)

➤ This is one of those ancient manorial sites that never developed. It is a tiny street running off the sandstone ridge, cutting between hedgebanks and trees and hiding most successfully from the hurly burly of nearby Guildford. Only the visitors to Loseley House are likely to fall upon it and indeed it is a further dimension to their experiences at the great house, for this is the estate village.

Sir William More-Molyneux bought Orange Court Farm about 1750. It was already old then for this is an impressive collection of farms and cottages from the seventeenth century, and earlier.

The house to note is Nos 8/9 which may well go back to the mid-fourteenth century. The end nearest the road displays a pair of eaves crucks which are a rare survival in Surrey timber framing.

In 1843 they built a school for the estate children, squidged right in the heart of it all. That's now become the church of St. Francis. Its little tower with short shingled spire is barely noticeable and so is a great surprise on peeping through the gateway.

Lower Kingswood

Ancient Byzantine art from Constantinople had found a home in this most unexpected place. Beside the roaring traffic of the A217 just north of the M25 interchange is a little mock Byzantine church built in 1891. It is dedicated to St. Sophia who has a far grander building in Constantinople but from that city a Dr. Freshfield collected sculptured capitals which he then used in the building of this astonishing little church with the help of architect Sidney Barnsley.

Even when its locked, the cheery herringbone brickwork and unfamiliar design give refreshing sights after the usual Surrey scenery. There's no integral provision for bells so there's a simple detached campanile to the north, complete with Byzantine folded dome of course. By the south wall stands an unused capital – not a very splendid one but better than total disappointment if you're locked out!

Lower Sunbury

'Sunbury, which is one of those pleasant villages lying on the Thames' wrote the famous naturalist, Gilbert White back in November, 1767 in one of his letters to Thomas

Pennant. He was recalling his visits 'about ten years ago' when he stayed 'for some weeks yearly' at the home of his friend the Rev. John Mulso. He was commenting on the vexed question of the time as to whether birds migrated. At Sunbury he noted the autumn gatherings on the osiers of the Thames' islands and wondered whether a Swedish naturalist was right in suggesting they hibernated under water. White actually favoured the migration theory.

The question has now been settled, the islands still exist, there are still osiers and Sunbury is still pleasant. It's much bigger and busier of course but it's still a pleasant walk under the trees along the river bank with the autumn sun shattering the views with brilliant reflections off the Thames' waters among all the boats.

Then the street begins as the main road inches between high riverside buildings giving an odd enclosed feel that's unique in Surrey. There are regular glimpses of the attractive cupola on the tower of a church that has proved easier to despise than to love. The headstones are distinctive for their extra large lettering. Then from the north-west corner of the churchyard the Old Vicarage can be viewed. It's odd. Where is the regular pattern of windows for this Georgian house? There are precious few windows at all. They haven't even been blocked. Was this house designed to evade the window tax?

There's a good old farmhouse next door, failing to hide its identity. Its stables and hay loft are now the garage of course. Next comes Thames Villas of 1887 looking exactly what they are and what a good terrace too. They're nearly untouched, even the doors. From those days of improved housing an aging builder's sign still shows through the whitening of a nearby house, including the service of 'sanitary engineer'. Inside toilets had come to Sunbury.

Little details give pleasure all around Sunbury. Here a Victorian wooden window carved from the solid wood, there some original casements, several different fire insurance plates, early plate glass shop front or an early petrol pump. The boatyard with slipway is always an interesting place but to find a gondola among the clutter was somewhat surprising although they regularly appear in old photographs of Thames water occasions.

A couple of more substantial items of interest could include Orchard House and Barclays Bank, both on the main riverside road. The former attracts attention for its architectural merit (c.1700) but much more important are the iron railings and gates along the street frontage. They're original and escaped being melted down for the war effort in the 1940s. The design includes the 'water leaf' motif where a scroll has been fashioned out into a wavy-edged leaf form. They seem to grow out of the very metal. In a sense they do, for they were forged or welded but not cut from sheet metal and so survive English weather well. Originally the idea came from Italy. During the eighteenth century this was the motif that dominated English wrought iron decoration. It practically ousted the more delicate acanthus leaf design that had temporarily flourished from its initiation only a few years before. The Tijou family, working at nearby Hampton Court Palace, had been the prime innovators for that.

Barclays Bank is dated 1888 and is one of those Dutch gable revival buildings that regularly occur in the second half of the nineteenth century and into the early years of the twentieth. Usually they are in hard stark terracotta red brick and tile but this one has been whitened and, when enhanced with a little sunshine, takes on a completely new appearance. It's easier to appreciate its small scale, good proportions and interesting detail. It is closer to what the architect saw evolving on the white paper on his drawing board. Surrey has quite a number of buildings in this style but for quality this must rate high on the list.

A little further east is No.47. I wonder how many people miss the two crude classical profile medallions up under the eaves, one on each side.

Lyne

Wallawaroo was the name of a sheep station in South Australia owned by a Scottish cooper, turned sea captain, turned sheep rancher. The name was too long for stencilling on wool bales and was shortened to Wallaroo. The owner, Walter Watson Hughes, discovered copper there and Wallaroo boomed through a whole variety of metallurgical industries into the sizeable town of today. Pioneer Hughes remained a prominent founder figure for over ten years and then, in 1873, sailed for England and settled at Lyne. He was knighted in 1880 and died seven years later, aged eighty-three.

His country house has survived demolition, unlike many in this region. It's Fan Court and has been in use as a school. That is something he may well have approved of since he helped fund the beginnings of higher education in Wallaroo. He's now buried in Lyne churchyard.

The churchyard has an interesting collection of headstones, unusual because so many of them tell something about the person. There's another Australian connection for example – Leslie Manifold Gorrie, born at Camperdown in 1887. He served as canon of Lahore Cathedral and chaplain to I.E.E. 1920 to 1947 when he came to England and became chaplain at Botley's Park until his death in 1955.

Botley's Park is another of the local country houses, surviving as an institution, as part of the National Health Service. It recurs on the headstone, to Sister Ann Leask, from when it was a War Hospital. Foxhills too, occurs on several stones. It is now a country club with notable golf course.

Another of Chertsey's old institutions is Sir William Perkins's School and here is remembered Mabel Annie Eastaugh who was Headmistress from 1913 to 1946, thus taking her children through two world wars. She died in 1971, aged 87. Several stones record the sons of the local big houses, who died at war. Locals may recognise the name Simplemarsh Farm on Joseph Vincent's headstone. Since he died in 1896 much of his land has been swamped by Addlestone. He's a link with another institution for he served on the first Chertsey Urban District Council.

Stones to Vivian Huntly Wolton and Anefre Moff are notable for having inscriptions in Greek, while Major General Frederick George Berkeley has a granite monolith. He lived at Almners and that house still exists (corner of Almners Road and Hardwick Lane). Parts are late medieval and it is usually said to be the house of the Almoner of Chertsey Abbey. However, a manuscript history in Chertsey Museum suggests the Abbey had great corn barns here for distributing alms to the poor.

Almners now has the M25 beside it and here the railway had to be carried across at an angle. That problem created a superb modern suspension bridge of which there is said to be none other like it. It is suspended from the centre and even there supports have had to be offset.

As for Pioneer Hughes; did he make a fortune out of his boom town? Judge for yourselves. He left £316,200.

Mickleham

An early type of aircraft is illustrated on a metal plate on one of the footstones in the churchyard (middle of eastern part). It commemorates Douglas Gilmour whose imagination was captured by the idea of flying and went to France to learn in 1909. He bought a plane and for the next two years clocked up a number of dare-devil exploits, such as roaring to Henley Regatta with his wheels touching the river. That soon had him in trouble and his flying certificate suspended but ignoring that, he flew on and crashed to his death in Richmond Park in 1912, still only aged twenty six. He is sometimes claimed to be the first man killed in flight.

For such a tiny place it's astonishing how thickly Mickleham's history is peopled with well-known names. There's over a dozen familiar ones before starting to count the lesser

Mole Valley below Box Hill, Mickleham.
G. Hawkins.

known. The key figures are well documented but in the village they've left little to remind us of them although a little brass under the church tower records the marriage of novelist Fanny Burney to French refugee General Alexandre d'Arblay in 1793.

The Saxon church was practically rebuilt in Victorian times but has gradually been enriched again. There's a stained glass window of interest to Canadian visitors and some Flemish panels finely carved about 1600 have been brought in to make up the pulpit. In the south transept is a beautiful sculptured profile of Queen Victoria to commemorate her Jubilee. It is the work of F. J. Williamson of Esher and in that town further examples of his work can be seen in Christ Church.

Opposite the church was stabled the Derby winner *Blair Athol* in 1864 when horses were stabled all around Epsom at race time. Hence the pub is called *The Running Horses*, depicting on its sign the Derby finish of 1828 which was a dead heat between *Cadland* and *The Colonel*. The former won the run-off and it is his portrait on the other side of the sign – according to local tradition.

Milford

The main roads seem to dominate this village but this is not new. They have been its life force for hundreds of years, giving rise to coaching inns such as *The Red Lion*. It brewed its own beer as was usual but during the 1890s had the distinction of selling it off in stone bottles made by Royal Doulton because the licensee was an employee of the pottery. When the local breweries began exerting a greater influence home brewing stopped and *The Red Lion* was taken over by the Broadford Brewery at Shalford.

A name that still prospers today is Courage and Mr. Courage owned Mousehill Manor. His butler left to become the landlord of the White Lion which was supplied by Hodgson's Brewery at Kingston. Ironically, that was one of the breweries taken over by Courage.

The oldest inn was built in 1540 and is now Chilston/Nine Elms Cottages by the church. Formerly it was the White Horse, a popular inn name because white horses were preferred for coaching as they showed up better in poor light. As a symbol of the Royal House of Hanover it later gained further popularity. The field where the coach horses were grazed was where they have now built the First School.

Milford grew in the nineteenth century like everywhere else but at an early date. It became an independent parish, from Witley, in 1837 and so has recently celebrated its 150th anniversary. Only Virginia Water is earlier (1831).

Molesey Hurst

Walk down Church Road in East Molesey and you look over the fields beside the Thames. Grayburn Way stretches ahead between what look like supports for a suspension bridge. Closer inspection reveals two sets of gates too wide to close the road. Only one from each pair does that. The other opens outwards into the fields, thereby demarcating a crossing place.

This is the former Hurst Park Racecourse which was last used on October 10th, 1962. Racing began on the Hurst at least as early as 1737 and became known as Hampton Races, the 'Appy Ampton Races' or 'Cockney Derby'. Indeed they came to attract large crowds, described by the end of the nineteenth century as 'considerable and not very reputable gatherings'. The end came in 1887 when the Jockey Club closed it down as unsafe. Undeterred, improvements took place but the Jockey Club would only grant another licence if there was one mile of straight course added. It was, and it was this that stretched down over Grayburn Way into East Molesey. These were re-named Hurst Park Races. The old paddock end is commemorated by a pub of that name. The grandstand was transferred to Mansfield Town Football Club.

Boxing, golf, cricket, they all have their tale to tell. Boxing first, from the bare-fisted days when this was the 'pugilistic Waterloo'. The English Championships were held here in 1805 and continued for a couple of decades. Vast crowds of 10,000 and more were reported as gathering then.

Less well supported was the first golf match ever recorded. Yes, it was against the Scots. The home team were English friends of the great actor David Garrick who was hosting them at his home in nearby Hampton.

Cricket has a royal history, having attracted enthusiasm from the Prince of Wales. He was Frederick Louis, newly of Hampton Court Palace, fresh from Hanover, on the accession of his father as George II in 1727. The first recorded match on the Hurst was on July 14th, 1731. Sixty-four years later the first recorded leg before wicket in England happened on the Hurst. Even the Australian touring team played here. That was in 1890.

It has certainly been a busy place. A flavour of the races was caught by Charles Dickens in *Nicholas Nickleby*.

Newchapel

➤ Who'd expect to find the London Temple out here? Having arrived, you can't miss it, right beside the main road. Not only is the whole complex very smartly maintained but was designed with some thought. There are open views as you might expect of a modern site but also some closed ones too with unexpected surprises and cheery with summer flowers. Next to the inevitable Surrey black and white work are unashamedly twentieth century buildings in brick and a dark tile but kept low and broad, unobtrusive yet self-assertive. Behind these is the white cuboid of the church itself, with white square tower surmounted by lantern and spire. That's the inviting view from the gateway and the Church of Jesus Christ of Latter Day Saints offers 'daily complimentary tours'.

Another eye-catcher is Horne Park Farm, not far along the lane to Horne. Its bright brickwork and stone dressings are very unfamiliar in Surrey but it's the domineering slate roofs that are really noticeable, with almost a hint of French architecture at first glance. It is all British nineteenth century and doesn't even look like a farmhouse. The matching farm buildings give the needed reassurance on that point but what a marvellous matching set. Not everyone will find it lovable but it's surely valuable as a representative of such individuality.

Newdigate

All you that pass this way along
Think how suddenly I was gone
God does not all a warning give
Therefore be careful how you live.

➤ So says the first headstone on the right as you enter Newdigate churchyard by the south gate. Oddly, the verse is offset to the right below the main inscription. Even odder is the contradictory second verse which has been inscribed over on the left:

> Afflictions sore long time I bore
> Physicians were in vain.

Then even the mason got confused and altered, by recutting, the last word of the next line:-

> Till God did please that death should (. . ? . .)

It looks like 'cease' now but initially was 'ease'. That, however, he needed for the next line which now reads:-

> And ease me of my pain.

But several of these words were re-cut into the first version creating a sort of stonemason's anagram. It is as though it was cut from dictation.

The church is well known for its timber tower supports but within the altar rails is another interesting item of wood easily overlooked. It's a monoxylem. That's just the fancy name for a dug-out chest. Look closely and you'll see why. There are no joints. It is one baulk of tree trunk with a thick lid over the chamber that has simply been hollowed out of the solid. Not so simple actually, as oak is a hard, dense timber even though medieval craftsmen regularly worked it green (unseasoned) in spring when the sap was rising. Then it was at its most workable. To defeat fraud there are three locks with three separate keys, enforcing the presence of all key-holders before the chest could be opened. Usually they were the cleric and both churchwardens.

The well-kept village centre is small but whichever way you come you will pass the outlying farms and cottages of which many are officially 'Listed'. Whereas many Surrey villages have their richest collections of architecture from the 18th and 19th centuries with just one or two early farmhouses, around here there are well over a dozen farmhouses from the 16th and 17th centuries. It is fine wealden vernacular work indicating, in part, changes in wealth and status hereabouts in those days. It was already becoming possible and popular to have 'a place in the country' as well as 'interests' in London. Alas the local church has no worthy monuments to bring those people a little closer to us.

New Haw

➤ Here the usual story of village church founding village school is back to front. The school came first, when local landowner, John Marshall Paine made a grant for a school for poor persons. A small stone room with lancet windows was built in 1874 and flourished. It served as a mission church on Sundays and that too flourished. New Haw continued to spread over the common and a larger school was needed, so in 1909 a new red brick one of three classrooms opened. Since enlarged, it still stands. So does the original schoolroom, for when the children moved out a chancel was built on to create a parish church. It was dedicated in 1911 but to which saint cannot be traced in the diocesan records. Nowadays it is known as All Saints but that makes it the second church of that name on Woodham Lane and so confusions arise. It's all very confusing anyway as New Haw merges imperceptibly into Woodham from an original nucleus at New Haw Lock on the Wey Navigation.

Street lights came in 1909; the first motor garage in 1911; the telegraph in 1912. The land was rapidly being developed. Much of it had been owned by Robert Fitzpatrick Escott of Ongar Hill House and thus 'Escott land' became 'Scotland' as in Scotland Bridge Road. The bridge is a hump-backed traffic nuisance, built in the eighteenth century when the Basingstoke Canal was built through here to join the Wey Navigation. The bridge was then called

Fullbrook Bridge and now that name has been revived by the nearby Fullbrook School.

Normandy

➤ Normandy is a scattered place that claims to have the most beautiful village cricket ground in Surrey. It's surrounded by trees and when viewed from the air is seen to be round. I can think of a few other villages that will no doubt hotly dispute that claim!

The tiny village centre is nearby but most of Normandy is scattered farmland, much of which was part of the great medieval Henley Park that stretched all the way to Guildford. Farming ideas and developments were tested here last century by a man who was a famous politician but who is now better remembered as the writer of *Rural Rides*. He was William Cobbett, born at Farnham, buried at Farnham but who actually died at his farm here. He is still remembered in local place-names. In his *Rural Rides* he revealed his sharp eye for good soils and good husbandry, his impatience with out-moded methods and his keen interest in profitable developments. His pen was equally sharp, flexing from scorn to praise to wrath but never fearing to express pleasure. At Normandy he tried to practise what he preached.

Not all changes in Surrey are for the worse. Here they decided to restore their pond which had become an overgrown swamp. Now it's a beautiful pool again with 81,000 gallons of open water, all due to the determined efforts of the villagers. On 5th January 1987 fifty volunteers turned up to begin the manual work of cutting, dredging and removing the muck. That lasted over several weekends until an area about 140 yds by 40 yds had been cleared. Apart from all this arduous work there was another equally vital side to the work – finding out how best to create a wildlife pool and recruiting the help and advice needed. Especially valued was the assistance given by the Thames Water Authority who provided a mechanical digger for two weeks for only a penny on the rates. Hopefully it will inspire similar projects elsewhere.

North Holmwood

➤ 'It stands well' announced my companion. 'You can tell he's an estate agent' I thought, but do you know, he was right. The church is well proportioned and well sited on a rise, backed with trees, from the rough grassland and two little ponds that lie between it and the road. There are pollarded willows too; not many of those left in Surrey. It all sounds rather attractive and indeed that view is, but around it the proximity of Dorking has spawned an insensitive rash of housing. Fortunately the terrain is undulating and much treed, so many buildings are out of sight. But even those with careful maintenance and much-loved gardens cannot compensate for the apparent lack of cohesive planning. Standing by the green, noting the older buildings and looking out over the trees and ridges to the Leith Hill range, it's easy to visualise how beautiful this location was once.

The open airiness seems to have infected the church architect too (Rhode Hawkins, who built the north aisle of Blechingley church). Inside he seems absolutely determined that nothing should punctuate the space. There are no arcades. The chancel arch is built so wide that it reduces the side walls to buttress proportions. There are no screens. Even the tie beams are banished from the roof and are replaced by mean iron rods. It resembles a warehouse.

Outside, the spaces are so carefully controlled. The flint walls are carefully quoined and attractive bonding-courses of brick run the eye along the south wall, and so forth. Most laudable was the decision, probably financial, that the flints should remain whole and not be knapped. Hurst Green shows how hard and ugly large surfaces of knapped flint can

124

be. Here though, the knobbly texture in soft colours is just right.

In complete contrast is Brickworks House down by the roundabout. It's one of those grand Jacobean houses in solid deep red brick with Dutch gable. Look more carefully and details reveal it is a modern imitation. No wonder it is so good; it was originally built by the Redland Brick Company for their own use. The street frontage is a fine advertisement.

The Nutfields

The development of this high ridge site has not created another Blechingley, alas. The ridge is narrow here so the communities slide down each side. The railway passed south and fostered South Nutfield which became a separate parish in 1888. The Nutfield to the north is the elder with a much altered and restored medieval church which caught the blast from a flying bomb in 1944. Restoration was completed in 1962.

Follow the lane downhill from the church and a mighty long terrace is passed. Two sections are much older than usual, going back to the eighteenth century and these were later (c.1870) joined. The gradient necessitates a broken roofline which adds considerably to the attractiveness. Further on is Nutfield Marsh, a wild and weedy place with a couple of picturesque buildings. It is so rough and rural yet right next door to the sprawl of Redhill.

Oakwood

Or Okewood if you prefer it! If you've explored the forest clearings containing Forest Green and Ockley then travel further into the Wealden forest to find this church (there is no village, just a parish of scattered homes).

When people spread out to live more permanently in the forest during the thirteenth century then this church was built. At first the people may have only have been present for parts of the year when they were exploiting their rights in the forest. Their church, although only one room, was as good as any other. It could afford expensive stained glass windows (fragments remain) and artists came to decorate the walls; Gabriel still greets the Virgin Mary in an Annunciation scene and St. James the Great still stands nearby. The de la Hales were the local family and Edward is still commemorated by his brass whereon he wears the 'SS' collar of the House of Lancaster. His house was at Wotton.

We still enter by the ancient oak door of two thicknesses with the grain laid in opposite directions to counteract warping.

It wasn't ever a really important place and it was sold off by Edward VI and reinstated by Elizabeth I. It's had famous benefactors too, such as John Evelyn the diarist, Dr Godolphin Dean of St. Paul's, and Sir William Perkins who features in the history of Chertsey where the school he founded still flourishes.

There is more to see and all saved by the Victorians who also enlarged it. It stands on the rim of a deep woodland dell, beset with bluebells in May and with white garlic all along the streamsides that cut through the scene. This all has to be negotiated to reach the church so it's not recommended for wheelchairs.

The garlic reminds us that, with onions and leeks, they were the most important vegetable of the country people, echoed today in the ploughman's lunch of bread and cheese and pickled onion. This was the staple diet for hundreds of years of such people as worshipped here.

Ockham

➤ In 1985 a new window was unveiled in the church. It shows, boldly and simply, a medieval Franciscan above the words 'William of Occam c.1285–1349 Doctor Invincibilis'. This local lad became lecturer in philosophy, theology and science at Oxford, promulgating that God could only be known by faith and not by reasoning. He was therefore a Nominalist rather than Thomist and his work laid the foundations for the Reformation and modern empiricist philosophy.

As part of the 1985 celebrations the Franciscan Institute of St. Bonaventure University presented Ockham with the collected works of William. It had taken ten years to collect together and amounted to seventeen volumes.

It's the usual scattering of ancient farms and cottages around but beyond the A3 is Ockham Mill (1862) at the end of a little lane. This is a remote and beautiful corner with a very striking watermill that's not of local vernacular architecture at all. Red brick enhanced with black glazed bricks worked in mock Romanesque style, it is quite a surprise. The millstones now pave the path across the lawn, glimpsed over the garden wall. Out of another wall a weeping beech droops over the millstream. The route continues over the fields, now as a footpath but once as a cart track to a wharf on the Wey Navigation. That has now disappeared. The associated buildings have too, being recorded only by nettles. As you cross the river though, lean over the parapet and down in the water you can spot the foundations for the old cart bridge.

Ockley

Practically every village can offer a few details about somebody who sounds interesting but there is never time to explore all of them more deeply. Ockley is such a place.

In 1638 the rector moved on after twenty years service. The next May he and twenty four others sailed from London to the New World to found Guilford in Connecticut. So says a plaque in the church about George Whitfield. What made the rector of such a tiny, remote, Wealden parish change his life so dramatically?

He left at a time of change. The old village around the church (presumed) was in decline and was regenerating further west along the London road. It's the modern A29 following the straight line here of the Roman Stane Street. Along it is strung a superb collection of seventeenth century homes and later ones of course, carefully spaced in a way no deliberate design could keep so subtle.

The impressive thing is the long narrow green, over half a mile long, stretching at a lower level than the road. Thus there are good views across it and just like the one at Forest Green it jostles uneasily with the forest for its place and the Leith Hill range guards it all dramatically as the background.

At the south end a trackway borders the green, beginning with one of the finer individual houses, all weather boarded. Then comes the school bearing the date 1841, hence its quality for it preceded the rash of brick and slate schools with lancet windows that became so standard after the railways came. Next comes St. John's Church, of that later period.

In the corner is a very picturesque old farmhouse, half-timbered with brick infilling, and so along the bottom of the green to another. A duck pond lures you on to another group and so off to the village well, under an incongruous roof on classical columns, looking rather silly now that it shelters a seat.

Ockley is fortunately a conservation area and so hopefully

will remain special. At least the S.E. Electricity Board was persuaded to bury its power lines out of sight in 1975. Back in 1700 the workmen were so proud of their new church tower that they had built that they boldly carved their initials into the buttresses. How many can you find?

Ottershaw

➤ Along the north side of the churchyard wall a gravelled road leads into the trees. Along here on the left you will find two former lodges to Ottershaw Park. They're worth seeing. They are not the usual Surrey-style brick and tile buildings, attractive but repetitive. Instead they are a century earlier (c.1795) by James Wyatt. This is not 'Wyatt the Destroyer' but Wyatt at his best.

Now smartly maintained, the white walls set off by the green lawns in their setting of trees and shrubs make this a beautiful neo-Classical corner in summer sunshine. It's easy to notice the soft grey Doric columns and imitation stone plaques but to miss the most interesting point, the plan. For each lodge comprises two squares joined at the corners so that the bottom left corner of one meets the top right of the second.

Outside their gates the old coach road runs back down into the village. There, the older buildings, like the village forge, are now disguised among the modern. In the shopping street, lower end, on the left, notice some small bungalows much older than anything else. They are said to have begun life as squatters' homes. Local tradition says that if they could build their chimney by sunset then the squatters could keep their piece of land. It's not so long ago that all about here was common land and the Park was well stocked with deer and trees. Much of its early written history concerns trees, even the name, which goes back to the early Middle Ages.

Outwood

It's quite astonishing how the Surrey landscape can change its character so quickly. Crossing from the lowland farmland around Horne to the higher farms of Outwood it is quite noticeable. Over 2,000 acres of land hereabouts has been given to The National Trust so it should still be there when you read this! Part of that large gift comprises Outwood Common, not a sandy heathland but lovely woodland on clay to which the public have access. Arriving in May, the side nearest the windmill was enhanced by flowering horse chestnuts and extra saplings had been planted which make this a distinctive corner. Stepping into the woodland it's a green world, pungent with the scent of hawthorn blossom and crushed water mint, chiming with the calls of chiff chaff warblers.

The grassy areas of the common by the roadside were patrolled by guinea fowl. This is definitely no ordinary Common. It's an added bonus for all those visitors who arrive on summer Sunday afternoons to view the post mill in action. Dated 1665 it is the oldest working windmill in England, positioned at the highest point of course to catch the wind. The western end has the sort of distinct development that Surrey can show to perfection – commuterism.

Oxshott

Stockbroker Surrey is a popular conception widely held outside the County. It's not true. Reading of the traditional farms and old cottages in this book should soon dispel that notion. Oxshott, however, is one of the few places that does indeed fit the stockbroker image and so it is worth seeing for that reason alone.

It is a late development and so there's very little to see of any age or interest. The sixteenth century highwayman's cottage in the high street wouldn't get a mention anywhere else.

The story of the development could well have been totally different. In New Road, Prince's Covets, is Jessop's Well which yields mineral water and back in the eighteenth century it was the scheme of Mr. Jessop to use it to foster the development of a spa and thereby make himself a millionaire. It all came to nothing because Epsom Spa beat him to it.

West of Warren Lane there is a war memorial marked on the street map. It's an unusual one, being dedicated to the boy scouts and it takes the form of one cast in bronze. This fine statue, in a field at the top of a track, was cast in Surrey by the famous foundry at Thames Ditton.

There's a little industrial archaeology of interest at the level crossing where two lines once ran side by side, necessitating two sets of gates in succession. One line is still in use but the other closed with the brickworks it served. Of that, a single gate remains and the trackway is all weeds. So is the site of the gatekeeper's house marked in 1987 by a lonely upturned bath.

Oxted (Old)

➤ Timbering, brick and tile, it has all the old Surrey village qualities but without the Surrey 'feel'. Even Ian Nairn found it 'oddly grim' when he wrote the Surrey volume of the *Buildings of England*. He likened it to a 'North Warwickshire mining village'. There is certainly something different about it.

The Downs roll along as a fine backcloth to the north and to the south the land continues falling away. Even by Spring Lane its a rural scene of trees and hedges and the attractive little valley of the river Eden. A footpath comes down from the village and brings you to a millpond, complete with ducks of course. Beyond, glimpses of red brickwork and white paintwork, materialise into a watermill running along behind the causeway over the dam. In fact it drops another level below the roadway so the view from below is of a building with very different proportions. This can be seen from the footpath that continues down the valley to the Hay Cutter pub. Another path runs up the other side of the pond so there's plenty of scope for exploring here.

Against the mill wall in Spring Lane five of the old millstones are leaning. Thus for once they can be inspected closely and their differences noted. Nearby is Mill Cottage, looking attractive but also deceptive. It's not as old as it would like you to think.

Peaslake

If you like single track lanes entrenched between high banks, roofed over completely with a summer-green vault, then this is the village to explore. It's high in the Leith Hill range with sudden vistas into blue or alpine type views down into fields that are little more than grassy clearings amid the millions of trees. There are real old farmyards, ancient cottages dotted about with Victorian villas and many present century homes. Everything is foiled and hidden among the trees so finding particular ancient farms, the Quaker cemetery or even the Victorian church can be a nightmare of ups and downs, twists and turns if you're not good at map reading. The walkers find the best of it.

It is this overall setting and style of development that is special here. Where else could you find such a place so near to London? In terms of Surrey villages it's so unlike the valley settlements along the Tillingbourne to the north or the forest clearings to the south that it needs seeing to complete an appreciation of the diversity provided by the county.

Peper Harow

➤ This is hidden Surrey indeed. It's a private park but access is permitted to the church. At the end of April when the buds are bursting and the pastures are emerald again this is a beautiful spot to seek a church. The private road off the A3 curves through spreading sheep pastures to the great Park House built by Sir William Chambers in 1763–1775. A purist can find fault but its sense of presence in its setting is worthwhile.

On its way to the church the road gives you a glimpse of the stables round three sides of the stable yard; a beautiful insight into eighteenth century life. Not all the bricks are of clay. Some are of the local Burgate stone cut in imitation; an expensive conceit but fun! Opposite the duck pond is the lych gate complete with coffin table, and beyond that some ancient yews.

The churchyard is walled and the old masonry is full of wild flowers. Against these walls now stand the headstones but the sloping churchyard is not bleak because all the memorials that cover the graves completely have been left and there are a lot of them. This is the most attractive of the Surrey churchyards of this type. Among those buried here is Sir Henry Dalrymple White who led the Charge of the Heavy Brigade at Balaclava.

The church appears to be Victorian but an original ogee window in the south wall reveals that parts are medieval. The nineteenth century work is in several medieval styles and yet it harmonises so well. That's because one architect, Augustus Pugin, did the lot (fascinating man; see Albury). Either he was trying to recreate the complexities of a country church or else he took his styles for each part from what was already there before his rebuilding. Certainly the chancel arch seems to have been Norman before he built the present imitation one.

In the chancel a fifteenth century lady is commemorated not once but twice. A cross and inscription mark her grave before the high altar where she wished to be buried according to her will. In addition there is a figurative brass and inscription where she is shown in widow's dress. Her husband, William Brocas, had died three years previously and was buried at St. Bartholomew's, Smithfield, London. Both of her inscriptions, despite differences in spelling, describe her as Joan Adderley. That comes from her first marriage, to John Adderley, who had been Sheriff and Mayor of London before dying in 1465. In both inscriptions someone at a later date has had the word 'armiger' added to show that William Brocas was important; he had the right to arms. Two shields of those arms were once displayed above the cross.

The road outside continues through marvellous traditional farm buildings out of the Park on the lane to Shackleford. There's a peep into one of the yards that contains a great granary built about 1600. You can't miss it. Twenty five wooden pillars raise it high above rodent level. It has the same sort of ideas as were used for Surrey's market halls, such as Dorking, Chertsey and Godalming, now all gone. It's all an astonishing glimpse into the past; the great park with its house, home farm and community church. Remember though, that all but access to the church is private.

Pirbright

I arrived here to find a real live elephant on the village green, and nobody else seemed to be taking any notice. Beyond stood the blue and white striped Big Top of a wandering circus. I wonder how much longer that entertainment can persist?

It is one of the most attractive village greens in the county, with cricket pitch and village pond complete with ducks. Tile-hung cottages, a few Victorian villas and some smart half-timbering complete the scene.

Leading off is Church Lane which confronts you with a giant monolith of Dartmoor granite bearing the odd name Bula Matari. That's the African name of John Rowlands, a Welshman. He went to sea as a lad, arrived at New Orleans and was adopted and given the name Henry Morton Stanley. Later, as correspondent for the New York Times he was sent by Gordon Bennett, the proprietor, to find Dr. Livingstone.

Eventually this soldier, journalist and great explorer returned to Britain. He was knighted, elected M.P. and settled in Pirbright at Furze Hill with his wife for the last few years of his life.

Off Dawney Hill to the north a lane leads to the Brookwood Memorial and War Graves (see Brookwood). It leads down an avenue of Scots pines – not the commonest choice of tree for avenues.

Out along the Aldershot Road is the Vokes Works hiding the ancient royal manor of Henley Park from view. In the nineteenth century it was owned by Henry de Worms who Queen Victoria created Lord Pirbright. With true Victorian ideals he and his wife became great benefactors to the village and were much regarded for it. High on the social calendar was their Christmas treat held for several hundred local children in the village school. However, in 1898 a new incumbent the Rev. Arthur Krauss, took office and shocked the village and the press by stopping the event. He was offended. Permission had been granted as usual by the School Board but it should have been sought from the Managers and Krauss was Chairman of these. Uproar ensued and lasted well into the New Year.

Lord Pirbright had the ultimate answer. He built the villagers their own independent hall beside the green and fast too. It had its official royal opening on May 31st by H.R.H. Princess Christian of Schleswig Holstein. It was a day of triumph and celebration but the festivities were a little quiet without the church bells welcoming Her Royal Highness. Krauss was striving for the last word. He pulled up the bellropes and locked the church. Another round of clamorous censure ensued.

The village hall still stands, boldly inscribed 'Lord Pirbright's Hall'. When he died he wasn't buried at Pirbright but at neighbouring Wyke!

Pitfold

➤ The Hindhead Hills run out in great spurs and scarps between the 'bottoms' into the Surrey and Hampshire lowlands. The Portsmouth Road runs off down one and immediately after Hindhead runs by High Pitfold. The village of Grayshott lies to the right.

Pitfold is just a district name for the hill with its scattered houses, gardens and woods. The Grove School was once Hindhead Court after being bought about 1910 as Hindhead Copse, by John B. Body. He had the small house rebuilt with twenty six bedrooms, completed by 1914. Attention was also given to the forty acre grounds and an impressive collection of trees and shrubs was built up, especially ericaceous ones that thrived in the acid sandy soils.

A great range of greenhouses provided for ferns, peaches, vines and carnations. There were also houses for tropical plants and cacti to remind him of his foreign travels for this was the man who discovered oil in Mexico, became Chairman of Mexican Eagle Oil and Canadian Eagle Oil until they were expropriated by the Mexican Government. He was partner to the first Lord Cowdray and built Vera Cruz Harbour and most of the railways. He died in 1940 but many of his trees live on and part of the shrub collection was moved to safety at Haslemere by his widow and daughter.

Further down the ridge there's the turning left into Hammer Lane and then again into Woolmer Hill. At the entrance to the Secondary School is an old house, Pitfold House. Here George Bernard Shaw spent his honeymoon, and fractured several bones. The house was lent for this occasion by the parents of Lord Beveridge. Shaw and local residents are brought to life by Flora Thompson, author of the famous 'Lark Rise to Candleford'. They appear in 'Heatherley', her fictional name for Grayshott, back up the hill and mostly over the Hampshire border. Here in 1897 she came to work at the Post Office for three years and listened over the counter to GBS expounding on Socialism. Customers from the Surrey side of the border came from 'the other settlement' – Hindhead.

Pixham

Surrey is full of unexpected little corners that catch the eye on driving through and this is one of them. It is totally unexpected when approaching from the A24 but slow down at the lowest point and you're crossing the Pippbrook Stream that once drove Pixham Mill, still standing to the right. In white weather boarding it nestles among the trees defying anyone to make derogatory remarks about nineteenth century industrial architecture. By the side is Mill Cottage, two centuries earlier, and a very picturesque building in white plaster between strong black beams. A little sunshine and a few summer flowers and what a picture it is!

Move on and there are more old cottages dotted along the lane, representing some three centuries and a little church of 1901. Waiting for the traffic lights to let you through the bridge makes you feel you've arrived somewhere. Pixham has a sense of place.

Puttenham

Even Queen Victoria thought that Puttenham was a beautiful place and so it is, sliding off the south flank of the Hog's Back where it catches the sun. The village street runs

137

down from the church and then uphill again with the usual selection of brick and tile and oak beams. There isn't much though that a visitor ought to see although in 1985 it seemed to be the last place where West Surrey's old tradition of growing hops still continued.

In church the good quality brass of Edward Cranford (died 1431) may be missed under its mat in the chancel. It shows the rector in full mass vestments. Another brass shows the arms of Francis Wyatt impaling those of his wife Timothie. She was a Burrell and her arms include four burdock leaves – not the commonest motif to be adopted into heraldry. Today the burdock is a coarse weed of wasteland. It was regularly introduced by John Constable into his paintings where it still looks like a coarse weed! It does have herbal uses and was even more valued in 1634 when Francis Wyatt died.

The two manors that made up Puttenham were bought and then mortgaged by General James Oglethorpe to help pay off the debts incurred when he was founding the state of Georgia in the USA. There is no evidence that he ever lived here or intended to. His home was Westbrook at Godalming.

There are good walks from here out over Puttenham Common and so around Cutt Mill Ponds. George Sturt recorded in his *Journals* for 1891 that he and a friend went blackberrying on Puttenham Common on 29th September. He was sick that night and all the next day. Of course he was. Surrey folklore warns that after 25th September the Devil will have peed over the blackberries.

Pyrford

Compared with many counties, Surrey has little of prehistoric interest to stir the imagination, except for the enthusiast. At Pyrford, however, is a standing stone around which, it is presumed, ancient peoples gathered for some form of worship. This is a logical presumption because at some later date it was Christianised with the embellishment of a Christian cross. Probably this was done before the Saxons built churches. Certainly for centuries it acted as a boundary marker adjacent to a field named 'Holy Cross'. Modern road widening caused it to be uprooted and discarded but now rescued, it stands in the verge opposite the south end of Upshot Lane. Don't look for something of Stonehenge stature though, it's quite small. Don't look at midnight either; it's said to get up and move around! It is also said to move about when the church clock strikes midnight. But the church has never had a clock!

> This is the true nature of Home
> It is the place of Peace . . . . .

So said the motto adopted by Sir Charles Dilke for his Pyrford home ('The Rough'). He's largely forgotten now but was once tipped to succeed Gladstone, under whom he was Under Secretary for Foreign Affairs. Unfortunately he was accused of an affair with the wife of another Liberal M.P. and his parliamentary career did not survive the ensuing divorce proceedings. He was a staunch supporter of the working man, the Trade Union Movement and the rising Labour Party. He came to Pyrford to write during the winter months and died here in 1911.

Ripley

◀ 'The pretty little village of Ripley' was where Sherlock Holmes spent a day at one of the inns before returning to Woking (*The Naval Treaty*). It's still a good centre to spend the day exploring the surrounding woods and farmlands of the Wey valley as did Conan Doyle, H. G. Wells and A. J. Munby. If you remember it as a place ruined by the congesting traffic on the A3 then fear not, for the realignment of that road has returned the village centre to more peaceful times. It has always been a busy place being on the main route to London. Its importance in the early days of cycling is well documented and the coaching inns, especially the Talbot, survive as reminders of early transport. On the same theme, the Wey Navigation runs out of sight beyond the largest village green in England, through its most rewarding point, at Walsham Gates.

Cross the green diagonally by the gravelled track and follow the path over the fields. Soon there's the roar of water rushing over the weir into a sweeping basin where the canal and the river part company. Between them is the lock cottage with its Wedgwood chimney pots. From here the lock keeper used to row local children across the floods to attend school in Ripley. Nowadays there is an extensive system of flood gates along the valley to try and prevent devastating floods. One set is here. Notice that the water on either side of the lock gates is the same level. Instead of serving their usual function these are only closed when it is necessary to prevent excess water entering the canal (because further down it runs level with bedroom windows) and the excess is thereby diverted over the weir.

Not being in constant use has ensured the survival of a very early design for these gates, perhaps the original design employed in the seventeenth century. The 'paddles' are raised and lowered not by a cranking system as on the other gates but by prising them up and down with a crow bar and then fixing them into position with a pin. Here

The Talbot Hotel

where the pressure is equal both sides no crow bar is needed.

The lock itself is not immediately recognisable because it's not the usual long narrow oblong. It is a square pool and that too is probably the original design. It has never had to be bricked and concreted like the busier ones and so the grass tumbles down to the water's edge as it always has but in a way that can no longer be found elsewhere. Notice the shallow steps for horses each side of the little bridge. There's much to find here out in the fields where cars can't get.

(Wheelchair access is probably easiest from the Pyrford side, by the track off the Lower Pyrford Road.)

Seale

➤ Lovers of Romantic poetry and Lord Byron in particular may be interested to know that he wrote the verse on the memorial to Edward Long in the north transept of the church. Soldier Long died at sea when his regimental ship, bound for Spain, had an accident with a man-of-war.

Nearby in church is a clarinet, a memorial to a sadly under-recorded aspect of Surrey's social history from the days before the re-introduction of organs back into churches. The villagers brought their own highly valued instruments to church, formed a band and provided their own music. Often it was an odd assortment of instruments and played with more enthusiasm than skill. Such bands were often at the back of the church, as at Seale and so the congregation had to stand and turn for the singing, hence 'to stand and face the music'.

Outside, the usual Surrey buildings are not quite so usual as there are several made from chalk blocks (not 'clunch' in Surrey). Although Seale has a famous chalkpit (managed by the Surrey Wildlife Trust) the chalk of the Hog's Back is usually too soft for such building blocks. It was normally reserved for lesser buildings and here it makes an impressive barn at Manor Farm west of the church. Just round the corner is Stable Cottage and that is quite an ambitious use of chalk. Elsewhere, chalk cottages occur by Broadford Bridge, Shalford.

Send

◂▬ Fancy visiting a mortuary? Perhaps that requires a stiff drink! Well, you can have both, for the *New Inn* by Cartbridge has been an inn since at least 1843 and the front single storey extension has also served as a mortuary.

It's beside the towpath of the Wey Navigation and the walk upstream to Worsfold Gates is the most interesting option. These gates are like those at Walsham and are the only survivors of their type (see Ripley). The black weather boarded buildings nearby are an old smithy and carpenters workshop such as can still be found in many Surrey villages. These are a little more interesting because it is believed they were built especially to serve the Navigation and so go back to the mid-seventeenth century. They are not open to the public but a typical smithy interior has been reconstructed in Haslemere Educational Museum.

Following the towpath provides an attractive walk to Triggs Lock and across the fields to Send church (often impassable in winter). It's a medieval church still retaining its pre-Reformation screen and this is the chief item of note. Such chancel screens closed the space under the chancel arch and thereby isolated the parishioners from the high altar. Two nave altars were provided instead, one on either side of the doorway through the screen, and these were protected by their own side screens. It is rare for these to survive in England but at Send the sawn off remains still clearly indicate this former arrangement.

In the churchyard is the large tomb of Lieutenant General William Evelyn, great grandson of John Evelyn the diarist (see Wotton). Its peculiarity is that the craftsman, Robert

Chambers, regularly signed his work in Hebrew. This Evelyn lived at Send Grove next to the church but although this has been a site in use since at least Norman times, no village centre has grown up here. The modern centre is beyond the ridge to the north east. The village is strung along the valley for a couple of miles or so from back at Cartbridge to Burnt Common. It is at the eastern end where the road crosses the stream at the former ford once known as St. Thomas's Waterings that the Cornish rebels had a confrontation with the Royalist soldiers during the 1497 rebellion (see Shere).

Shackleford

◀── Surrey is never monotonous. Here again is a village quite distinct from any of the others, largely due to its setting. Narrow lanes creep into and round the valley of the narrow river Wey which cuts deeply into the meadows. Up above it, on the north slopes to catch the sun straggles the village. Most of the homes and farms are old. Even the newer ones are probably on old habitation sites for many are dotted in isolation and not squarely aligned with the road, just as they would have been hundreds of years ago. Individually they are nothing special but sequence them out into Shackleford's succession and they make something special that could be so easily overlooked in searching for the particular.

For the particular I would single out the galleting: the insertion of small chips of ironstone into the mortar. It's a practice that goes back to at least 1630 in Surrey but its meaning is lost. Some say it was to keep evil out because by encircling the bricks or stones, rings of iron are created through which no evil spirit would pass. There are many examples here.

At Shackleford lived Richard Wyatt who built the almshouses at Farncombe but his home here has been rebuilt. Another house of note was built by Voysey in 1897 out by the church where it has become the district name of Norney.

144

The church is away from this part and more impressive than one would imagine on hearing that Sir George Gilbert Scott built it in 1865. From the village one approaches the west front and very imposing it is too, without being pretentious. It's firmly regular and yet not boring because the proportions are so satisfying. Another very satisfying view is from the lower part of the churchyard looking up at the north east angle of the tower – massive, impressive, yet not overbearing. This must surely be his finest church in Surrey. I couldn't get in; neither could the electricity man who'd pinned a card on the door wanting to read the meter!

Shalford

The interest here is scattered between four centres instead of the usual one or two. Motorists may well be familiar with the enclosing borders of terraces and cottages that line the main Guildford road in the proximity of the church. Visitors seek this point in order to reach the fine old tile-hung watermill operated by the National Trust. Other motorists seeking their road junction will look out for the large common cum village green, a wild and airy place in contrast to the former spot, with houses scattered mainly along one side. Then there is a little group of pub and cottages and factory site where another busy road crosses the River Wey/Godalming Navigation. Here at Broadford Bridge there is an access point to the towpath for waterside walks through the meadows. Fourthly comes a once busy corner that has sharply declined and that is the old Stonebridge Wharf. Here the Wey Arun Junction Canal branches from the Godalming/Wey Navigation. This was a busy place until the Guildford-Horsham railway line put the Wey Arun out of business. Now the canal is closed off, leaving just an arm for houseboats coming off the Wey Navigation. If the efforts to restore the canal are fully achieved then this

site may once again develop. For now it's a hidden nook down a footpath under the trees.

Back in the main street, the timbered cottages, disguised under plaster, are very attractive. The grey slates of some make a distinctive change from the usual Surrey tile. The stocks survive by the churchyard wall (others at Abinger and Alfold) but the church is a Victorian replacement of the medieval one.

To that one came an incumbent called William Oughtred. We've all had to learn how to cope with one of his little inventions. It's the X we use as a multiplication sign, for Oughtred was one of the great mathematicians of his day. He collected together what was known about arithmetic and algebra and published it in 1631 as *Clavis Mathematicae*. It became a standard text. He was tutor to Sir Christopher Wren but as he died in 1660 he didn't live to see his pupil's application of mathematics in architecture. From Shalford Oughtred went on to serve at Albury where he was incumbent for fifty years.

Another notable incumbent was David Railton who took to the Dean of Westminster the idea of the tomb of the Unknown Warrior. The Union Jack hanging over the tomb is said to be that used as a pall in France when Railton was burying the war dead.

More cheerful are the plant pots and window boxes often at the cottages by the church. This is not merely fashion but one of the village traditions. Back at the turn of the century Shalford was noted for its window boxes. Long may it continue.

From the same period comes the Methodist Church which was registered for worship on 23rd July 1895. Behind it stands their hall which is in fact the earlier chapel, inscribed 'Weslyan Chapel 1843'. Methodism spread to Shalford from Guildford and made greater headway there after a Mrs Attfield arrived in 1829. Her husband, William, became chief trustee of the Shalford Chapel.

Shamley Green

Despite the impression given by some guide books Shamley Green (formerly Shamble Lea) is worth a visit. There's a large green, cut by lanes, still giving the impression of an airy open space because the buildings are strung around the perimeter. No single building is likely to command your attention but nearly every one has something to reward a closer look.

Just off the eastern corner, up Woodhill, is the Old Barn showing where the central ancient part has been modified by succeeding generations. Beside it stands Barn Cottage which is only a section of a once larger house. The gable catches the eye, it's simple and effective with supporting crown post and that supported by braces, all in plain black and white. Notice that the bargeboards, to protect the ends of the roof timbers, are original.

Over the way stands Tanyard Farm, also of the seventeenth century although it is the brickwork of the next century that is noticeable. There's a good group of contemporary barns with it, in black weatherboarding, Surrey style.

Continuing anti-clockwise, Brook Cottage gives the impression there's timbering behind the tile hanging. Walnut Tree Cottage comes from the phase of stone-end buildings (fireproof around the hearth). The Court House is large but then it was three cottages. Note the base at one end being made of ironstone from the local hills. It shows clearly how the brick frontage is only a facade over the half timbering showing at the end. This enabled the owner to keep up with the Joneses when brick came into fashion but was too expensive for a total rebuilding. The adjoining barn is worth a second look too.

In complete contrast is the Forge next door. It's not great architecture but is definitely pretty and adds an extra style to the variety. It is not the individuality but the collectivity that counts here.

Further round is Chapel Cottage which looks quite an ordinary cottage, but the door and the side wall explain its name. The chapel began in 1870 I'm told. There used to be nine village chapels in the Guildford Congregational Group but this one, with Compton and Blackheath have been sold as private houses.

Arthur's and Arthurs Cottage are from the sixteenth century timber-framing days but isn't their positioning odd, one to the other? How close and complex were the medieval groupings. Also timber-framed is Potters, down in the corner. Here we can see how the later idea of raising the windows into dormers had to contend with the wall plate of the framing. It couldn't be cut away so it still passes across each of the windows.

Plonks and Plonks Farm are lovely names and indeed are more fine old vernacular buildings, on the way up Guildford

Road to the church. That dates from 1864, is pleasant enough but like so many Victorian churches it has received interesting gifts. A phoenix greets you on entry. It is of batik work so whether you like the whole banner or not, each square inch is a fascination of colour and pattern and texture. In complete contrast is the simplicity of a wood sculpture of the Mother and Child. Again the craftsman really understood form and medium – see the sweep of the wood grain flowing through Mary's lap and spilling down the rest of the costume. It's dark and smooth and beautiful.

Shepperton

Arrive by water, as in days of old. Many ferries used to cross the Thames even within living memory. Now one has started again, that crosses over from Weybridge to Shepperton Lock; a place busy with boats and people. Waterways seem to go off in all directions or plunge over the great weir by D'Oyly Carte Island.

There is indeed a connection between this island and the famous operas. The father of Rupert D'Oyly Carte bought it for a summer annexe for the Savoy Hotel but then found the authorities wouldn't grant him a licence. He decided to live here himself and thus his son's friends came to meet and rehearse.

The village is further on and suffers from the busy B375 so Church Square is often overlooked for want of a parking space (free car park further on). It's worth a little effort to come and explore. The little Thames-side village seems to have attracted more than its fair share of familiar names down through the ages, from Erasmus to Charles II and Nell Gwynne, from George Eliot to George Meredith.

From Church Square, walk through by Warren Lodge to Ferry Square on the edge of a great loop in the Thames. From townscape to riverscape, it is quite a surprise. If it's a quiet time the ducks will have moved off but they still keep

149

a hungry look-out for visitors. They fly in from all directions to splash down at your feet in case there's a snack on offer. There are Mallard and Aylesbury and smart black ones with white bibs. This piece of manorial land was given over to public use in 1970. The white manor house (c. 1830) is behind the wall. More rewarding is to peep through a wrought iron gate at Old Ferry House and its garden.

Back to the church and how admirably its scale harmonises with the square. Owing to a flood which finally ruined an earlier church nearer the river, this one was built in 1614. It's the only Surrey church from the time of James I; there aren't many in the whole country. A tower was intended but not built until the patron, Queen Anne, visited and demanded one. So the present tower was built in 1710, with brick. It's not red Surrey brick but Thames Valley brick of mottled subtlety. Sunshine and wet change its colour daily, sometimes reddish, sometimes nearly lilac. Notice it is oblong in plan.

Notice also the external stairway to the west gallery, added in 1834. That's another national rarity but does occur again in Surrey at Shere. Even rarer is the second outside stair to the manorial pew.

Inside, the west gallery carries Hanoverian Royal Arms. That's not unusual except that these are painted directly onto the panelling. If they are contemporary then they'll be William IV's and there aren't so many of those about.

Below are 19th century box pews; yes, 19th century box pews. Everywhere else the Victorians ripped out box pews in favour of pitch pine benches but not here. Just to further confuse you they are not square-topped but have traditional fleur-de-lys carved ends like medieval benches. They fill the nave but the spacing seems odd anyway. That's because the proportions are so broad that the overall plan approaches that of a Greek cross.

Outside, against the north wall is the sad headstone of 1826 to a 10 month old baby. She was Margaret, daughter of the Victorian poet and novelist Thomas Love Peacock who has many local connections (e.g. Chertsey and Lower Halliford). It was he who composed the verses on the head-stone: 'Long nights succeed thy little days . . . The too fair promise of thy Spring'.

Another flood reminder occurs around the corner towards the High Street. There is a 'prae' (local dialect) or raised footway above road/water level. Russell Road branches off here. It is named after Shepperton's longest serving cleric, the Rev. William Russell who spent 53 years saving the village from its 'depravity and immorality'. Look up the High Street and you'll see a church window. That's his but it is a school not a church. It was founded in 1833, long before the Education Act, but Russell didn't wait for Parliament. Education was needed so he gave it, in the Rectory. High on the school wall is an inscribed stone commemorating the family. Easier to spot is one for the 1st Shepperton Scout Group, 1936 and yet another says 'The ground two feet outwards from this wall belongs to the school estate'. Only part of the school survives but it was made attractive by incorporating the school house into the design.

Opposite is Glebeland Gardens with a good 1899 terrace of that name in cheery red brick, still little altered. Other Victorian homes here are worth noticing. Rosemary Cottage props up an enormous ivy just like we see in Victorian illustrations.

Shere

◀ The church guidebook simply says, 'A second brass on the chancel floor commemorates Lord Audley'. What a tale that keeps hidden!

This Lord Audley was Sir John Touchet who came into public service with the new king, Edward IV, in 1461. By 1466 he was worthy of the grant of this manor when its owner fell from favour. His career survived the troubled reigns of Edward IV and Henry VI, the reign of eleven weeks by Edward V, and after the accession of Richard III he became Lord Treasurer, in 1484.

John Touchek from his brass
Sketched from
A Hawkins 11.8.89

His skills at successfully playing political games were not passed on to his son James. James co-led the Cornish Rebellion of 1497 against the policies of Morton and Bray, acting for the new king, Henry VII. As the insurgents marched from Cornwall to Kent they passed through Shere. It must have been impressive as there were reckoned to be 15,000 of them although there are indications that the total was far fewer. For this little adventure James was beheaded for treason on June 28th 1497 and his peerage became forfeit. Ironically, the king gave the manor to the very minister James had opposed, Sir Reginald Bray, a great national figure. The manor has remained with that family to this day, hence all the Bray memorials in their chapel in the church.

Fortunately John Touchet had died a few years before his son disgraced the family. His brass was not cut until about 1525.

In the east window of the Bray chapel pieces of very fine medieval glass survive. An eagle, symbolic of St. John is particularly striking. The other evangelists have their symbols surviving too: Matthew's angel, Mark's lion and Luke's bull. (The only other fourteenth century set is at Oxted.) Also in the window is a very noticeable chequered shield. That was of the de Warennes, for long the Earls of Surrey. Their lives make interesting reading on a winter's evening as they too played the political games.

From the church a footpath crosses the Tillingbourne Stream and joins Gomshall Lane where you are far more likely to find a parking place than in the village centre. Shere is usually reckoned to be the most attractive village in Surrey. It certainly has hundreds of visitors.

Shottermill

A woman who didn't dare be one came here. A woman novelist was not quite respectable in Victorian times, not if she was to be taken seriously. Thus Mary Ann Evans published her work as 'George Eliot', was indeed taken seriously and now ranks second after Charles Dickens. Her great Masterpiece *Middlemarch* was largely written here in a little rented cottage called Brookbank. It has now been extended and the newer half carries that novel's name. You'll find it on the hill between the church and the railway bridge.

The railway wasn't built in her day. The view was then over woods and fields which she and her 'husband' George Lewes would walk together each evening. Mornings were for writing. She sat at the window, feet on a hot water bottle, all shrouded in woollens, fearing the cold. Only

Brookbank, Shottermill. G. Hawkins 1985.

when heat stifled everyone else would she concede to feeling a little warmth and venture to work in the garden. Below ran the Wey tributary that is the County boundary and beyond that Mr. Shotter's mill that gave its name to what has become a suburb of Haslemere.

South Holmwood

◣ Just like North Holmwood this is another place that escapes most of the guidebooks. It shares the same hilly treed setting and again the church sits smartly on a hill. It has an attractive exterior. The architect of the tower followed the local wealden stone style so there is a friendly familiarity about it. Several architects created this church last century and inside it shows. The arcades, in good imitation Early English, fail miserably to do anything more than stand in a great space because the aisles are so wide. This width is currently highlighted by the lack of furniture in the south aisle. The nave benches are an insult to our national tradition of good church woodwork and design. The south aisle windows are ill-proportioned for the wall they penetrate. Happily, the chancel is more successful (by J. B. Watson, 1838; his only Surrey work is St Mary's, Staines).

Outside, the stops to the hood moulds over the south aisle windows break away from the usual motifs. Although the oak and acorn do occur elsewhere, ferns and holly seem to be represented too. Is this influence from the Romantic Movement drawing inspiration from the local natural setting?

The little lanes about here have another smattering of development. Much is hidden in a dell and all the more attractive for that. There are enough Victorian ones to show the growth of the hamlet and a big non-Conformist chapel of 1874.

South Holmwood is on the 1867 railway line and by 1888 a Surrey guide commented that the common was 'being rapidly built on'.

Stoke D'Abernon

What a marvellous French name to approach on the signboard. It's enough to fill any village explorer with thoughts of Norman England. Here though you can't find the village because it hasn't the sort of development typical of Surrey villages. It is easy to drive right through. Never mind, go back and opposite the Garden Centre there is a Victorian lodge and a driveway down an avenue of fine trees curving round wide lawns.

At the end is a church, a Georgian Manor house and a farm, all beginning to fulfil expectations. Peep over the churchyard wall and there is the River Mole gushing over a low weir and the idea of the original riverside setting begins to take shape.

Imagine a happy honeymoon couple wandering together along here and your fancies will have more truth to them than expected. Here took place the earliest recorded honeymoon. The bridegroom became a national figure of great importance for he was William the Marshall. Even at the time of his marriage he was great enough to secure the hand of the heiress of the Earls of Pembroke and a wedding in Wales could not be agreed upon. It took place in London instead and a Norman knight called Enguerrand D'Abernon lent his manor house at Stoke for the purpose of a honeymoon.

That was back in 1189 the year that Richard the Lionheart came to the throne. Inside the church there is another reminder of that reign. It's the enormous chest, one of the finest of its kind in England. Some people will point out the slot for receiving coins and suggest it was made for collecting the King's ransom in 1193. He'd been captured on his way back from the Crusade. In 1199 further efforts were needed to free Jerusalem from Muslim control and so chests were ordered for churches to collect more money. This may be one of those.

The interesting point is not its age but its construction. Early chests were hollowed out of baulks of tree trunk. That way they had no joints to prise apart and the church valuables were secure. This chest however, shows the invention of joinery and how security was maintained.

The front is one surface of three interlocking planks with no room for a burglar's jemmy. He would have no luck at the ends because those panels are set back and reinforced with thick cross-battens. The front of the lid is secured by iron locks and the hinges cannot be forced because there aren't any. The lid works on a pivot cleverly concealed inside. The bottom can't be forced down because that too is fitted up behind the planks and it won't be weak with rot because the vertical planks are extended to lift the whole chest clear of the damp floor. It's all very clever.

Finally the carpenter took his simple tools and created intricate roundels of carving on the front. They must be Surrey's earliest wood carvings.

Nearby are England's earliest brasses that attract so many visitors including the Sir John D'Abernon who entertained the King and royal court at his Manor here on May 29th 1305. The Manor has been rebuilt since then of course. The present one, east of the church dates from c.1760 but incorporates parts of its 16th century predecessor.

Stroude

◄ This motley collection of houses along the road from Virginia Water to Egham will make you wonder why it's been included. But do look again. Look at No. 388. It is an old farmhouse, set at an angle from the road, attractive with its lawns and screening trees. One end is white, the middle still rosy brick and then a fascinating Gothic end, well maintained in white weather boarding and smart black paint work for the frames etc. The pointed windows have leaded lights and the roof is of harmonious tile. You will wonder what it was; chapel or school or an ornate stable for isn't that an air vent in the roof? It's more fun to wonder than to know!

Then in 1901 they built three villas opposite. At first glance they don't seem worth a second but look again. They're untouched. The double glazing agents haven't been successful here – the fenestration is original. The doors are original; one has been stripped but tastefully. The brick-work hasn't been painted and central heating hasn't put paid to the chimneys. They've still got their chimney pots too. Sights like this are being swept away every day making this all the more precious.

Now you've got your eye in, wander up the road. The houses mostly date from the period when it was fashionable to incorporate a name and date stone. Thus it is possible to work out most of the sequence for the development of this hamlet – 1880, 1883, 1887 and so on. You'll come to one odd one (No. 425), narrow and sort of slipped in. That's dated 1909. Who said 'infilling' was a modern necessity! It shows developments too with emerging bay windows and two tone brickwork.

That's enough of being nosey. Other people's homes can be left and one of several footpath signs followed out into the fields for a different exploration of this corner of Surrey.

Sutton

It's on the lane up from Abinger Hammer to Holm-bury St. Mary. It is too small for a sign but you cannot miss it because there's a largish black and white half-timbered house right on the bend. Just below it is another timber building but this time the infilling is brick. Over the road is one more, looking older. It's black and white again. Then there's a pub which has a large garden climbing the hillside. From there it's a fine view down on to this tiny grouping. It is worth seeing because many corners of Surrey must have been like this before Victorian times. Nearest is Holmbury St. Mary which was also tiny before the Victorian 'outsiders' discovered it. They created a new parish, uniting the hamlets of Pitland Street, Felde (now Felday) and Sutton to create Holmbury St. Mary. *The Surrey Volunteer*, I'm told, commemorates the general idea rather than a particular recruitment.

Sutton Green

For his services in France at the Field of the Cloth of Gold, Sir Richard Weston received the manor of Sutton from Henry VIII. Later, when the house had been rebuilt the king came as a guest and three years later executed his host's son for being implicated in the Anne Boleyn scandals.

The rebuilding of Sutton Place created the first great English house to lack fortification. It is also one of the first houses in England to use terracotta for ornamentation and there's much more Renaissance work of interest for being so early. The plentiful vine leaf decorations have given rise to the story that Weston was the king's wine merchant. This is not true. He served as Gentleman of the Privy Chamber and Under Treasurer of England. He was also Knight of the Bath. (At the time of writing the house was not open to the public but there had been announcements that it would soon.)

The surrounding Park, and farmland, is much reduced in size compared with the original grant. Portions had to be sold off to retain solvency when a later Sir Richard (born 1591) was in national disfavour for being a Roman Catholic recusant and for being dubbed a royalist after recruiting support from Charles I for a scheme to make the river Wey navigable (see Stoke-by-Guildford). Thus in 1641 the portion at Clandon was sold to Sir Richard Onslow who created Clandon Park (see West Clandon). The farmlands of today owe much to Sir Richard Weston who became an agricultural pioneer as well as a canal builder. He introduced clover from Brabant and Flanders to enrich meadow grass with

Canal Scene
West Surrey.

protein and to put nitrogen into the soil. Thus the clover features on one of the village banners. There's not much to the village, just a few old farms and a little modern housing. The old tin mission hut has been rebuilt and there is a quaint, rather domestic-looking, modern church. From Sutton Green there is access to the rural walks along nearly twenty miles of towpath of the Wey Navigation. Sir Richard had died just a few months before his scheme was completed. It had taken over thirty years to get approval and less than two to build. It's one of the earliest schemes in the country and now in the care of the National Trust.

Tadworth

➤ The B290 road through to Epsom Downs from the A217 snakes through the village centre and that is the main feature to see here. The road continually changes direction and gradient, giving a succession of changing views so that although the buildings are modern the experience is not boring. Compare it with nearby Banstead and the difference is startling; the latter is bleak while Tadworth has a human scale. Compare it also with Ashstead's main road street and appreciate how good that might have been.

The focal point on this route is the station. Enthusiasts of railway architecture may be interested in this one for being so late. The Chipstead Valley Line, built in the 1890s, was not extended through here to Tattenham Corner until 1901. The viaduct over the road beyond the station may also be of interest.

Tandridge

➤ Touring around Surrey you'll soon be aware of the Victorian architect, Sir George Gilbert Scott, at places like Ranmore, Shackleford and Busbridge, and also there's St. Pancras Station or the Albert Memorial in London to recall. He lived nearby and his wife is buried in the churchyard with her carved marble tomb chest under the yew tree.

The aisles of the church were added by her husband but fortunately he didn't ruin the woodwork. Step inside and one is immediately aware of it, as the enormous timbers supporting the belfry stand in the nave by the door. The oldest go back to about 1200 but the massive structure would be impressive whatever the age. It's odd that we're more likely to be impressed by this, which utilises gravity, rather than by a stone vault that defeats gravity and requires so much more engineering skill to achieve.

The roofs of about 1300 catch the eye too because dormer windows have been inserted through them. Thus the light filters down through the trusses making stark silhouettes of some and shadowy patterns of others.

Tatsfield

◤ There's a very odd district here that makes an interesting comparison with the Garden Village area of Woldingham and with part of Dormansland too for that matter. The roads on the map turn out to be narrow rutted tracks cutting down through the woods with a whole variety of housing tucked along them, buried in the trees. Evidently it grew up as a 'shack colony' in the 1920s in association with nearby Biggin Hill. Some of the corrugated iron homes survive, far smarter than shacks though.

Back in the eighteenth century, John Corbett thought very highly of his parents – according to the monument he erected in the church. His mother he describes as 'Exemplory Virtuous' and his father, a 'carpinder', was 'truly ingenious'. John was a skilled craftsman too for he describes himself as a Painter-Stainer of London. (Painters worked on wood; stainers worked on cloth). John Corbett presumably worked with wood like his father, for the monument is of that material. He would have painted it convincingly to imitate marble but his marbling has gone now. Nevertheless it's a handsome monument. I wonder how deeply John was involved in the dispute his Livery Company was having with the Heralds over the right to paint arms. It was some dispute. In 1712 when the monument was erected it was in its 124th year!

Tattenham Corner

Far beyond Surrey this place name is well known as part of the Epsom race track. The railway was extended up to here in 1901 so the architecture for that is late and the community that has grown up around it, modern. More absorbing are the old photographs taken during Derby week, showing rows of steam trains in the sidings, waiting to take the race goers home.

The downs are open airy places for walking, with vistas over London from the northern edge beyond the grandstand. That's not so during the first week of June – Derby week. Then the downs are obliterated with all the travelling people, the showmen, the food vendors, all those involved with the races and thousands who come for the occasion. You'll love it or you'll hate it.

The most widely documented Derby was on June 4th 1913 when all attention was on the horses rounding Tattenham Corner. Suddenly a woman broke out of the crowds, rushed onto the course, and throwing her arms up, was run down by the king's horse. Police Constable F. Bunn was on duty there and although he saw her rush forward she was too quick for him. By the time he reached her she was quite unconscious but not killed as too many books now say.

She was taken by motor car to Epsom Cottage Hospital where on Sunday 8th June she died from her injuries. She had been identified as Miss Emily Wilding Davison from Long Horsley in Northumberland and at the inquest two days later the West Surrey Coroner Gilbert H. White, recorded a verdict of 'death by misadventure', not suicide as is often reported nowadays. Her half-brother told the inquest she was a 'militant suffragist' and that he thought she did what she did to attract attention to the suffrage movement. She attracted no sympathy from the royal family; "horrid woman" wrote Queen Mary.

Thanks to the events occurring in the age of photography they have become the second best known historical event in Surrey, after Magna Carta. The scene is not as Emily knew it

163

for the grandstand complex was rebuilt almost immediately afterwards. Little of the old remains. Behind the stands is the Derby Arms and on its front elevation has been painted a large portrait of 'Diomed – winner of the first Epsom Derby'.

Thorpe

► Driving here you will probably worry more about scraping the high brick walls than anything else. It's like Petworth, Sussex, for nowhere else in Surrey is like it. They're the old estate walls which have been retained since homes and gardens were created behind them. Other cottages have built walls along their frontages too. It gives an identity and distinction to the place; so obvious yet so easily disregarded.

There are many fine old buildings about the village and most of the modern ones harmonise. Turn off into the little church square (rather like Shepperton) and you'll find a particularly varied group; timber and brick, tile and slate, even a rare example of Surrey thatch.

Thorpe was held by Chertsey Abbey until the Dissolution. As the Abbey was dismantled it is no longer possible to study its craftsmanship so a visit here is necessary to see the north and south chancel windows. They are of a standard superior to that of their neighbours and so probably by Abbey craftsmen. They are from the 14th century, a good time for the Abbey and evidently for this church too for there are other indications inside of quality refurbishing. It is a pity this church receives such scant attention in the guide books.

In medieval days the chancel was screened off from the nave either side of the central entrance through the screen. Their positioning here meant that masonry blocked the view of the High Altar in the chancel. Thus when a priest was officiating at the nave altars he couldn't see east, couldn't synchronise his service with that in the chancel at the Elevation of the Host. Consequently windows were cut through the masonry. With their decorative cusped heads these are far superior to the usual square 'squints' and the only ones like it in Surrey.

The churchyard has a couple of local peculiarities. One is the work of a local mason who decorated his headstones with spirals (east side of church path). The other is the use of iron for grave markers (against east churchyard wall). Despite rust and damage they still survive; an increasing rarity.

Nearby is the village hall. Now they're not usually worth looking at but this one happily preserves a seventeenth century barn. It is not a Surrey type weather boarded building but a smart brick one. Just look at those lovely rough hand-made bricks. Some make little buttresses running up the sides. Between are the windows, narrow lancets in attractive groupings of three. This is definitely the village for brick. Visit on a sunny evening when the warm pinks and reds glow and the local yellow mortar enriches the colour further.

Thursley

◄━ The clerk who rose to be the Director of the Liverpool and Victoria Friendly Society was buried here in 1929. He was John Freeman, better known as a poet and critic, winning the Hawthornden Prize in 1920. He loved the countryside hereabouts and so in 1932 eight acres were bought as his memorial and given to the National Trust. Thus farm fields still butt the churchyard wall and help to create the rural setting of this beautiful village. Its unaffected simplicity surely pleases most visitors. Fortunately there aren't too many of those.

Whether or not you normally visit old churches this one is worth the effort. Stand by the altar in the chancel and you're standing in the same volume of space that the Saxons created. You can still peep out through the same tiny windows in the thick walls as they did during the good weather. On other days they could blot out the chill and damp with sheets of horn or oiled cloth and the wooden frames for this purpose are still there as they are nowhere else. Later, when the Normans came they liked it too and painted lines and flowers in the window splays. The red paint is still there today.

At the bottom end of Thursley village street by the little triangle of grass is the house where Sir Edwin Lutyens grew up. Thursley gave to him his understanding and appreciation of the time-honoured building traditions and materials. When working with these he produced some of his finest houses such as Tigbourne Court over near Witley. His mother and nephew Derek are buried here at Thursley.

166

Dotted all around are fine examples of the vernacular architecture he found so inspiring. To find them can involve some beautiful walks, especially as thousands of acres of the surrounding commons belong to the National Trust with open access. Chief of these is the Devil's Punch Bowl which can be reached by the old drovers' track from Thursley. Plans were announced in 1987 to alter and maybe even re-route the A3 which curls round the rim of the Punch Bowl, so there could be major changes in this location, especially if the proposed viaduct is ever built.

It is still possible to follow the course of the old coach road on which occurred the murder of an unknown sailor, which is a famous local story, who is buried in Thursley church-yard. Recent research disputes the accuracy of the names and details on the various commemorative stones.

Tilford

'In a hole called Tilford, down Farnham way' growled George Bernard Shaw after not enjoying a country walk. He was not tuned to the delicate squelch of mud nor to the wild and woody landscape blurred by falling rain and as for the bird that 'laughed' at him from the woods, that prompted an appreciation of why some folk shoot such things.

It's a great cricket centre and a beautiful place to come and watch it on the sloping uneven triangle of village green. It's so uneven that losing teams complain that the batsman cannot see the bowler begin his run.

A member of the Haslemere cricket team was Sir Arthur Conan Doyle and when he came here his imagination saw a very different battlefield. He put Nigel Loring's Manor House in the vicinity of the church and looking down the green to the river he saw the colourful array of Edward III's knights and squires trying to take the bridge from Loring's men. It's all fictional romance but good reading, in *Sir Nigel*.

Conan Doyle's other local historical romance is *The White*

Adding mathematical tiles to a granary during restoration.

Company featuring Waverley Abbey. In reality it was the Monks from there who almost certainly built the two early medieval bridges over the Wey; either end of the Green. They are two from a series of identical bridges along this part of the river and possibly date from 1233 when great floods destroyed the existing bridges. There is little architectural detail from which to date them. Sheer simplicity is totally in keeping with the Cistercian Order's interdict against decoration.

They are not without interest though, for only in this series can you see semi-circular cut-waters (on the downstream side). The reason for this innovation has not been explained.

The river always runs well here. It is the confluence of the two branches of the Wey, one from the sandstone hills at Blackdown, Sussex and the other from the water table of the Hampshire Downs at Selborne. Between them they maintain such a good flow that there are said to be more water mills per mile on this river than on any other.

Now children play in it. Instructive books for children were written by Charlotte Smith who died here in 1806 and has the church reredos to her memory. Over at Lobsworth Manor by Black Lake lived J. M. Barrie from 1900 to 1909 and thus Black Lake became the centre of Never-Never-Land in *Peter Pan*. The village hasn't grown up either – there's no modern development.

Titsey

Come to it from the north and enjoy stunning vistas from up on the downs. It's a totally different landscape from those seen from the West Surrey viewpoints and so obstructed by trees.

Dropping down the lane, Titsey is easy to drive past for it is just a hamlet yet it has a large Victorian church. It's a familiar story. The old church was in the park until the

arrangement proved unacceptable to the park owner who built a new one outside (see Albury). It was Sir John Gresham, the eighth and last baronet, who caused the change but of course he did remember to transfer the monuments of his notable ancestors from one church to the other.

The church is still owned by Titsey Charitable Foundation who open it at summer weekends and Wednesdays. They also allow access to parts of the park.

Church Cottage opposite usually gets a mention but personally, I found Forge Cottage and Titsey Court on either side more appealing.

Tongham

A change of village centre scenery occurs here. The explorer is confronted by a pair of preserved oast houses on the corner of Grange Road. They are square based, instead of the familiar round, and rather short, but a valuable survivor from the days of local brewing and when the lands in this part of Surrey were primarily devoted to hop fields. These oasts date from 1858.

Just up the street towards the Hog's Back is the village hall, built to commemorate Queen Victoria's Jubilee. It gives the impression that appearances were important, that only the best would do, and so the brick frontage towards the street is richly ornamented, incorporating the foundation stone of 1897 and an inscription on a brick relief urn recording the official opening on 26th May 1898 by the Lord Lieutenant, Viscount Midleton. It's a bright red splash of village pride that makes modern halls look very dull and utilitarian.

The church (1865) has the distinction of a detached bell tower. The timber one, held up with iron rods illustrated in older guide books, had to be replaced nearly forty years ago. There's now a brick successor which is also oddly skinny.

Virginia Water

➤ Alphabetically speaking, most of Surrey has been visited by now and it clearly doesn't deserve its national reputation as 'the Beverley Hills of London'. Virginia Water is one of the few places worth seeking out because it does promote that notion. It's not especially noticeable unless you explore the residential district to the west of the village centre. Try and approach by say Abbey Road from the end of the shopping parade and so out towards Wentworth.

It's all so discreet, so rich with trees and free from pavements and kerbs, lines and signs. It's a pity some of the recent estates found in Surrey haven't taken ideas from here or at least reduced the restrictions imposed upon householders to prevent them from enhancing the sacred 'open plan' where only the wind enjoys the impersonal void. After all, it was right back in 1902 that the Garden City man, Ebenezer Howard, published *Garden Cities of Tomorrow*. But as we all know, tomorrow never comes!

Unfortunately the same care has not been lavished on the service areas of the Village. Outside the railway station is as desolate as any other.

The shopping parade is very obvious with its mock Tudor work, although the central section with upper balconies is carefully done. Despite its respect for local style and materials it still looks self-conscious.

For complete naturalism try the nature trail beside the river Bourne (go down the hill from the station traffic lights). There you can explore a typical piece of Surrey damp oakwood with great bumps of tussock sedge and the chance to spot the gaudy mandarin ducks that have naturalised out of Virginia Water Lake (See also Stroude).

Virginia Water Lake & Valley Gardens

➤ This famous beauty spot in Windsor Great Park was dug out and created by soldiers from the Battle of Culloden for the Duke of Cumberland, victor at the battle, and Ranger of the Park. The designing fell to his deputy, Thomas Sandby, helped by brother Paul. It is a beautiful and popular place to explore.

Everyone seems to enjoy the waterfowl but note in particular the Mandarins, not that the multicoloured drakes could be missed. This colony spread out and began naturalising the surrounding countryside early in the century. So successful have they become, together with those naturalised from a few other private collections, that they have now been added to the British list. Few birds achieve that. Mandarins didn't even breed in Britain until 1834 although they were introduced back in 1747. They nest in hollow trees, which seems odd for a bird with webbed feet, but will also adapt to special nesting boxes.

Most of the attractions in this Surrey-side of the Park are well known; the Azaleas and Rhododendrons particularly so, in their season. Few admirers realise how special the collection is though. Since 1918 J. B. Stevenson had collected Rhododendron species in order to study their groupings for classification purposes. He amassed hundreds including the Rothschild collection which had outgrown Exbury and came to Stevenson upon Rothschild's death. In turn, in 1950, Stevenson died, bringing the problem of finding a new home for such an extensive and valuable collection, the finest in the world. King George VI came to the rescue and so by 1956 some 2,000 plants of over 430 species had been successfully moved here from over the Berkshire border.

They now form a prime attraction in the Valley Gardens. These rank as the finest woodland gardens in the country. It is also the last great adventure in the modification of natural landscapes having been started in 1947. Notice how subtle the influence of man appears to be; no formal elements here. The mastermind behind it was Deputy Ranger Eric Savill.

Also here is the Kurume Punch Bowl lined with the small-flowered Azaleas originating from Kurume in Japan. In 1920 E. H. Wilson brought 'The Wilson Fifty' back to the west and we've been developing new clones ever since, especially in the U.S.A. So that's another fine collection that has been made a home here and brings a blaze of colour in Spring.

Even in winter there is interest. Apart from the beauty of the landscaped woodlands, it's a good time to appreciate the evergreens, the hollies. There are more than you think, over three hundred species in the wild, not all suited to our climate though. Of those that are suited, a national collection is being developed here.

Walton on the Hill

In the mid-twelfth century a craftsman took a rectangle of wood and carved along it an arcade of four round-headed arches on spiral-decorated columns like the masons built in Durham Cathedral. Within each arch he carved a seated figure. Above and below was added a decorative frieze. All was cut sharply in high relief because it was then pressed into damp sand three times to repeat the figure up to twelve. Then it was cast in lead and rolled up to make a font depicting the twelve apostles. It's the earliest surviving lead font in the country. There were only about thirty others because church law decreed fonts should be made of stone. At some time this one was cut down to only eight and a half arches.

The manor house is said to contain parts of the oldest domestic house in Surrey but much of the village is Victorian which excited some writers. The wild weedy corners leave me wondering whether what was there before has been spoiled. Even the village pond has been concreted around. The little green by the church does make an attractive corner. It's still a place difficult to imagine in Tudor times when Katharine of Aragon, Anne of Cleves and Jane Seymour were associated with it. Queen's Wood still survives.

Wanborough

Wanborough is a gem. There's so little of it that few people stop to look. From up on the Hog's Back all you can see is a tiny church, a manor house, a couple of homes, a farm and the surrounding fields. In other words it remains today just as most other Surrey villages began. Nowadays we have to remove all subsequent development in our imaginations. Here you don't need to – yet.

The great weather-boarded barns are most impressive by the entrance. They owe their existence to the monks of Waverley Abbey who had their vast sheepwalks on the downs behind. Being Cistercian they were permitted to employ lay workers and how busy it must have been here at shearing time, as fleece after fleece was stacked high in the barns.

Once a royal manor, it was sold to Gilbert, Waverley's second Abbot, back in the days of Henry III. Six monks were then dispatched here. At the Dissolution, Henry VIII sold the Abbey and Wanborough to his Treasurer, Sir William FitzWilliam (Earl of Southampton, Lord High Admiral etc.).

The manor house next door has had its moments too. Its good red brickwork must have pleased an exponent of the virtue of brick, King James I. He and his Queen, travelling this way from Loseley to Farnham, stopped to take refreshment and ended up knighting their host in his garden.

Last century brought more important guests. Gladstone's government held cabinet meetings here because the tenant was Gladstone's Parliamentary Private Secretary, Sir Algernon West. Even Queen Victoria came. Although the railway was built north of the hamlet in 1847 it wasn't entirely convenient for these meetings because there was no local station. Never mind, Sir Algernon was Director of the London and South-Eastern Railway and so a station was soon built! It was opened in 1891 and called 'Wanborough' but is in fact over the boundary in Normandy.

Into this century and the political connections continue with Asquith becoming sub-tenant. Two of his daughters are buried in the churchyard. The church itself is a single cell from the 13th century, sensitively restored in 1862 after being out of service for some 200 years. During that time it was used for storage, workshops etc. Once again it's clean and peaceful in this quiet corner.

It's a secret corner too. During the last war the house was the operations centre for the French Resistance Movement.

Waverley

◀ The Borough of Waverley takes its name from a large and important Abbey, the ruins of which are now open to the public that stand on the banks of the Wey. The spot was deliberately chosen for its remoteness and even today it appears to be in the middle of nowhere. Details of its history and of the remaining masonry can be found elsewhere but a few extra points may be useful.

Its real importance lies not in it being the first (1128) Cistercian House in England but that it was Cistercian. Unlike all other Orders, these operated under central control maintained by the Mother House at Citeaux in France. General chapters (International conferences) were regularly held and thus this organisation could share news and expertise with an unparalleled efficiency. It made them the foremost enterprise in Europe and at such Chapters it is said that pre-eminence was given to the Abbot of Waverley.

'To work is to pray' was a belief that set them maximising the potential of their lands and sharing their developments,

especially technological, among themselves. Metallurgy, leather-working, wine production, water power – region after region shared the advances of its speciality, England led with sheep and wool.

The daily allocation of six hours to manual labour was not enough so this Order permitted the employment of lay brothers – a highly profitable innovation. At Waverley the vaulted building was the dormitory and refectory for the lay brothers. Notice it is well away from the Monk's dormitory which was the fine building in the opposite corner. If you have ever wondered how stone vaults were constructed, part of the lay brothers' vault has been robbed – leaving a clear sectional view.

In the remaining block of ruins you can step down into a rectangular room with a stone seating plinth along the walls. This was the chapter or meeting house. Notice it's not polygonal as in so many other monasteries; that refinement to aid communication had yet to be fully utilised. Note also that it is between the church and the dormitory, not the most convenient for attending the obligatory night-time services, especially in winter. This design was soon abandoned in favour of siting the dormitory next to the church, often linked with 'night stairs'.

The Cistercians and Waverley rose to great importance. Thus on December 16th 1225 King Henry III 'entered the chapter house and at his own request was admitted an associate of the Order'.

West Byfleet

Rosemount and Lavender Park Road conjure up dreamy scented summer days that seem well-suited to city folk who created this dormitory village. Needless to say, it wasn't quite like that. They built their houses over fields of flowers that supplied a local distillery with essential oils. They swept that away too and built another close. All that remained were memories of using its upper room as a social centre. Pay 2d. a week and have a friendly cuppa over a game of dominoes to the shriek and rattle of a skittle game.

It's the rattle of traffic now, but West Byfleet isn't what it might have been. Dartnell Park does have houses in it but back in 1899 it was advertised for 58 building plots and 27 shops; the Old Woking Road was due for 46 but less were built there too. It's a wonder there's much development at all because there was no station built when the line went through in 1834. It had to be added in 1887. Then of course they needed and built a Railway Hotel. That needed a licence which was granted but at the expense of *The Sun*. Having lost its licence *The Sun* continued as a residence for a couple of years before being demolished. 'Sun Cottages' perpetuate the name just as Highfield Road records the days of open farmland when it was easier to appreciate the land falling away all around.

West Clandon

When Sir Richard Weston of Sutton Place was down on his luck and trying to create the Wey Navigation, he had to sell off part of his estates. That portion became the smaller Clandon Park, seat of the great Parliamentary family, the Onslows. It's now a National Trust property and thus well documented.

The village street is very long with the usual old Surrey buildings strung along it plus examples of commuter villas since the railway passed through in 1885.

A rare gem in the church is a pre-Reformation wooden panel showing the patronal saints, Peter and Paul, aside St. Thomas of Canterbury. Maybe it was once an altar piece. More probably it was once part of the dado of the rood screen. In either case it is the only Surrey survivor (those at Thames Ditton are from the upper schemes of the rood). Today the paint is faint and flaking but still the faces of the old faith look out.

179

Westcott

➤ People who let their livestock escape were a curse and so a village 'pinder' was appointed to catch animals and impound them in a special enclosure until the owner had paid a fine and was allowed to retrieve them. Nine such pounds survive in Surrey and one is here at the bottom of the green by Pound House. It's eighteenth century.

The street continues with quite some variety. For complete contrast compare The Barracks with its richly coloured and textured walls of natural materials (17thC.) with the smoothly plastered Old Mill House (early 19thC.) which has been colourwashed pink like something from Suffolk. The street has the rare distinction of retaining much of its rural character with narrowness, grassy banks and hedges. Only in a few places have these been breached and a frontage sub-urbanised.

Little hint of this is given by the Victorian development by the main road. Sir George Gilbert Scott appreciated the character when he built the church in 1852, on the hillside overlooking the village. Unfortunately he was not at his best with the interior. He took the fourteenth century ball-flower motifs and stuck them round the soffit of the chancel arch like light bulbs on fairground architecture.

Talking of fairs, George I granted John Evelyn the privilege of holding fairs on his Westcott manor. These were for each year on 15th April and 28th October.

West End (Chobham)

➤ A roundabout and the Gordon Boys School sums up West End for many people but there are some attractive corners to find. Down in the south east corner of the green the villagers restored an old pond so that it is now attractive with lilies and other water plants, sheltered by trees and rich in wildlife. Benners Lane runs nearby and just to the south it passes Malthouse Farm, a textured study in warm brick and tile. Opposite is another large house with many differences to enrich a few moments here. Follow the lane out to Beldham Bridge and there is an eighteenth century farm group; smart little brick house, weatherboarded barn, still all rural. The lane back towards Chobham via Pennypot is also rural with another eighteenth century farm at Hatchgate. There's also a turning down to a ford for those who still enjoy the simple country pleasures.

Gordon Boys School preserves the memory of General Charles Gordon (1832–85) who earned the sobriquet 'Chinese Gordon' when in command against the rebel Taipings. He is perhaps better remembered for ending a ten month siege at Khartoum when trying to evacuate Egyptian forces during the Mahdi's revolt. Today the school has a museum relating to his life but it is not generally open to the public.

Today we expect the pupils to live out their schooldays but in the churchyard is a sad row of headstones to those of an earlier age for whom such an expectation was less certain.

West Horsley

Somebody with far more patience than I have has counted 109 quarries of stained glass leaded together to make an exquisite medallion only twelve inches across. It shows the martyrdom of St. Catherine and was made at the beginning of the thirteenth century. It is of national importance and can be seen in the left hand lancet of the east window of the parish church. The gleaming wheel of her torture still glows out amid the rich blues and reds. Apart from its early date the artistry of the design would win it acclaim. Another contemporary panel but without quite such a strong sense of design, showing Mary Magdalen washing Christ's feet can be seen in the central lancet. The third, to the right, is modern. Surrey also has one of the

nation's earliest glass pictures of all. It's the Madonna and Child at Compton, probably installed in the final phase of building the Norman church. Unlike these it is no longer very clear.

Turn to the north chancel window and there's another panel of medieval glass. It too is clear, obviously a 'donor panel' but this bears the name of the knight kneeling in prayer upon the chequerboard tiles. He's Sir James Berners (the stone effigy of one of his kinsmen lies beneath him) who was a favourite of Richard II and acted as one of his advisors – Richard was only ten when he was crowned. His advice however was not impartial and so James was accused of taking advantage of the king's youth but it was the Peasants Revolt that gave the excuse for his arrest and execution on Tower Hill.

Sir Walter Raleigh was another of West Horsley's executed knights and his widow lived in the great house opposite the church, treasuring the head of her husband which she somehow managed to procure. It's now in the family vault beneath the chancel. The church has much else of interest but one other intriguing item is the ladder in the tower. It must surely have been put in place as the tower was being built because it's too long to get in afterwards. Therefore it must be thirteenth century and the tower built up around it.

West Humble

◣ Ruins are a rarity in the county, partly due to the lack of good building stone. At West Humble a tall flint gable rises out of the vegetation beside the lane. Visible foundations mark out a rectangular building with the stumpy base of the opposite gable. This was once the village church, back in the twelfth century but even by the close of the Middle Ages it had ceased to serve a need. Now West Humble Chapel is in the care of The National Trust, adding a further reminder of the ever-changing patterns of life in the countryside.

Burney House, Burney Road, Camilla Lacey, are all reminders that the eighteenth century novelist Fanny Burney moved here from Great Bookham. Their new house, Camilla Lacey (subsequently burnt down) records nearby Polesden Lacey and her novel *Camilla* that funded the new house. Her sojourn here is well recorded in her *Journal* and there is still a great downland landscape all around that she loved so much.

West Molesey

◣ Cholera swept London in the 1840s. The Thames water was suspected of carrying the disease and so in 1852

Parliament banned it for household use unless collected from above Teddington Lock. Thus the private water companies operating at the time moved to the Molesey/Dittons district to collect their water. They came unstuck again because they thought only about the Thames and overlooked the Mole and Ember rivers which cross this area and proved most consistent at clogging waterworks filters with their silt. The companies had to move their sites but they had come to stay. Storage reservoirs were built after the 1870s, right up to recent times, to operate upon an inexpensive gravitational feed system. Thus they had to stand above ground level and so to approach West Molesey from Walton necessitates skirting great embankments holding back millions of gallons of water.

Much of West Molesey's environs have been drowned for ever, yet beside Walton Road the eye catches a glimpse of the old days, passing an old barn, big and black, with extending catslide roofs each side of the central entrance. The tiles have gone. They've been replaced by slate and even now these are sagging. It is to be hoped that somebody will save it.

Next door, no.403, is a really rich piece of architecture; a three bay house of early date with compound chimneys on both ends giving a good balanced picture with the simple Dutch gabled porch with recessed oval in the centre. It is the best thing you'll find around here.

A little further on is Grovelands. The Grove in Walton Road was the home of the Rt. Hon. John Wilson Croker, M.P. To him is attributed the introduction of the name 'Conservative' for the Tories. He hated reform. He retired from Parliament because he didn't get his own way resisting the repeal of the Corn Laws. He also helped start the famous Quarterly Review and therein he would speak his mind without interruption. Soon he had made bitter enemies in the literary world as well as in politics. John Keats suffered in particular. On the credit side, he did buy a farmhouse and give it to West Molesey as a vicarage because they didn't have one.

184

Next comes the church and another surprise. It is of 1843 but retained its late medieval stone tower in the Perpendicular style. Despite early beginnings for this style in Surrey (see Effingham) the County has only two good towers, that at Stoke-next-Guildford and this one. Even so, it's very modest compared with its contemporaries in East Anglia or the West Country.

Further on is Molesey Football Club and this is indeed a spot to contemplate progress. Here in May 1785 you would have been among the spectators for something quite incredible, a hot air balloon. How astonishing it must have been tethered above the spectators' heads. They had done it in France two years before and now it was our turn. Member of Parliament William Wyndham and James Sadler climbed aboard and up they went, making Sadler the first English aeronaut. What a journey to France it would be; pity they landed in the mouth of the Thames!

Windlesham

━━▶ Visit the Nursery Garden Centre of L. R. Russell and you're visiting another historic site. Garden centres had to begin somewhere and this is believed to have been Britain's first, when the present owner, Mr. Louis Robert Russell returned from America with the idea and persuaded his father to let him try it. Mail order was declining so it was worth trying and now such places are all over the country.

We only see the Garden Centre, which is not unlike hundreds of others, but behind it lies the cumulative knowledge and expertise of three generations of Russells, each of which has received the highest honour we can give in horticulture. That's a unique achievement.

They have provided dozens of new plants to grace our gardens. Have you got a large leaved variegated ivy on the wall at home? It's possibly *Hedera dentata variegata grandiflora* which was discovered on a wall at Richmond,

London, and has since received the three highest awards possible. Perhaps you have a fine leaved rose covered with sprays of little single yellow flowers very early in the summer. It was bred in 1946 and called 'Canary' but just before judging it was discovered that the name was already in use, so we buy it today as 'Canary Bird'.

Here you can also buy 'the best Viburnum on the market' called 'Anne Russell' after the present owner's mother. It was granted an Award of Merit in 1957 and in the same year won the Cory Cup for the best new plant of the year. It was bred by Mr. William Little by crossing *Viburnum Carlsii* with *V. buckwoodii* and was a classic success for it combines the best qualities from each parent. Nowadays it is a favourite all over the world from Holland, Germany and Italy down to New Zealand.

The Russells moved here in 1936. One of their former nurseries has new fame for Twickenham rugby ground has been created over it.

Wisley

━━━ Nearly half a million people visit Wisley every year so you would think little would remain hidden. However, they pour into the Royal Horticultural Society's gardens and leave the little village beyond relatively peaceful. There's quite a variety of cottages and farms along the lane that goes on to the river, the canal and so to Pyrford. Between the two waterways it bends sharply through a farm and here's the place to stop. The farmhouse itself is attractive and tucked behind it is a gem of a little church; one of only two complete early Norman churches in the county. The other is over near Croydon at Farley.

The thing to see is the nothingness. There's just the church, the farm, the farmhouse and the surrounding fields going down to the river. Even in Surrey it has escaped development and seems to have been of this pattern since

186

Norman times. Even longer, in fact, for there's a prehistoric settlement site nearby and from there came the dug-out canoe now exhibited in Weybridge Museum. Wisley has had its grander moments though, when all the horses were stabled here during royal visits to Byfleet Manor over the river. It has seen national heroes like the Black Prince come riding by. The royal family still come but to the Garden. This little corner remains traditional, complete with wet and muck in winter; lovely!

Witley

When visiting pubs there are other things to think about than the architecture and at a first glance the White Hart does look like a typical Surrey mock Tudor effort. It is really far older. Parts go back to the fourteenth century which is not quite so surprising when Richard II's badge was a white hart. He gave the manor to his nurse, who was married to his tailor but the royal connections go back even further for this is thought to be the site of a building in which royal courts were held. Edward I was here in 1305 for example.

A tiny village out in the clayland forests seems an unlikely spot for such events but it is conjectured that an early road through the Wealden forests ran through here. One would have been needed to link the important royal castle at Guildford (King John's favourite) to Shoreham Harbour for reaching English lands held in France. The main coast road still cuts through Witley but unlike places such as Bramley the village has retained many older buildings in its heart, a conservation area, and one retaining its sense of townscape. There has been little twentieth century development here.

The White Hart has associations with George Eliot who lived at Witley Heights for a while, enjoying the birds' dawn chorus and planting melons in the garden. Here she wrote her last novel *Daniel Deronda*. Near her home is King

Edward's School wherein the Admiralty developed radar for the battle of the Atlantic during the Second World War. The school had been evacuated to the workhouse at Hambledon.

Woldingham

➤ The Garden Village is East Surrey's nearest equivalent to Virginia Water in the west. The expensive housing in a richly treed setting over the convolutions of the downs is worth finding for being exactly that. It's not all pretty-pretty either. There are still unmetalled roads, like Long Hill, with downland flowers drooping over the edges and a superabundance of trees and shrubs. The village hall is a total surprise and a reminder of much humbler beginnings to the district.

Driving south through affluent suburbia the green is another unexpected surprise with its very long and varied row of older buildings lining the far side. As a backdrop they keep the eye roving to and fro across the green creating a sense of peace as well as place.

Many organisations with intriguing names have left their mark in Surrey and here you can read that the Metropolitan Drinking Fountain and Horse Trough Association provided the fountain on the green.

Although the tiny church of St. Agatha is heavily restored it's still a delight and the church of St. Paul in the village centre is worth a look too. Built in 1933 in the Perpendicular style (pierced parapet, flushwork, etc.) it obviously hasn't weathered enough to look late medieval. It doesn't look Victorian either for imperceptibly the later period has left its mark. It is singularly appropriate too, looking thoroughly smart and at ease in its suburban setting.

Wonersh

➤ 'Green Place' is a mellow weathered half-timbered building by the roadside, in which lived the Elyots. They were among the local families involved in the cloth industry and we can see their brasses in the parish church opposite the house. Henry Elyot's brass shows no less than twenty-three children.

Wonersh is often referred to as the place where woad was grown as the dye plant for the famous blue cloth produced in this area. The woad fields, some at least, were not so much here as over at Unsted. Elizabeth I tried to ban the growing of it because it reduced her import duties on Italian dyes.

More recent village life appears as bas-relief friezes under the arch to the public open space by the church. This was all part of Wonersh Park, high walled to retain the deer that were still here last century. The walls have now been lowered and the Grantleys gone from the Park too. They are still commemorated by the Grantley Arms. Look carefully at the highest window in the gable overlooking the street and you will see that it still has its Tudor wooden frame with little arched lights.

Along the road opposite is 'The Friendly Free Church by the Common'. It's a sound building with polygonal apse at the east end but inside, the focal point is the west end where stands the pulpit. There are no galleries, just a sense of enclosed space created by the curved braces of the open timber roof over seating that is no longer in rows.

It's a far cry from its origins about 1860 in the kitchen of Great Tangley Manor. Overcrowding soon forced them out into a converted barn which was painted by a Mr. Seth Smith after he bought Little Tangley in 1867. His painting hangs in the porch of the present church which was built on land donated for the purpose by Mr. Smith. There's another painting of his, of the new church, but he must have worked from the architect's drawings because it shows a coloured tile roof which was never actually provided.

Originally it was a Congregational church but in 1972 became a United Reformed church with the union of the Congregational and Presbyterian churches.

The view outside is over to a hill. The roof among the trees atop it belongs to the house where once lived Thomas Cook of travel fame.

Worplesdon

◄ The dominant building here is *The New Inn*. New indeed but going back to Tudor times. Here the coachmen retreated during church services and to call them back to collect their employers from church a bell was rung from a turret over the stables of the rectory. That house has since become 'Maryland' but the bell turret was removed and added to the top of the church tower.

The church contains much of interest including some very fine medieval stained glass. A panel depicting a monk is particularly attractive. More important is a panel showing the Arms of Henry VIII and Anne Boleyn. These would seem to be the only Royal Arms in glass now in Surrey for Henry VIII, since the panel at Chertsey has disappeared sometime this century.

There is also a portrait of a former rector, the Rev. Duncan Tovey who was an authority on the poet Thomas Gray. His son was Sir Donald Tovey the music scholar and Reid Professor at Music at Edinburgh, but probably best remembered as a broadcaster.

Wotton

◄ Welcome to Wales! Anyone finding the narrow lane down the hillside will arrive at a medieval church with a

Gwent and Surrey towers for comparison.

tower design straight from Gwent. There it is a local peculiarity (e.g. Skenfrith) but occurs elsewhere in the Borders (e.g. Clun, Salop).

Enter the porch and the 13th century doorway is even rarer. The arch has been chamfered back so carefully as to leave eight little projections which were then carved into busts. They are showing their age now and the lowest two have been renewed. Tradition has it that they commemorate the fuss over the election of Stephen Langton as Archbishop of Canterbury. His head appears with Pope Innocent III, plus our Papal Legate, Cardinal Pandulf with King John and Queen Isabella.

The churchyard is left rural but the tall grasses and wild flowers are trampled around some of the headstones. Here music enthusiasts have come to visit those bearing the names of Vaughan Williams. Other pilgrims have worn a path round to the north east corner where a brick mausoleum has been built on. It houses memorials to three generations of Evelyns, including the famous diarist, John

Evelyn. He was born (1620) in the family house across the main road from the church. Around it remain some of the garden features he promoted. He helped bring evergreens into fashion and wished to be buried under the laurels in his garden, or failing that, in the church but definitely not in the mausoleum.

Wyke

Pronounced wike, not wick as in some counties.

'There's a princess buried in the churchyard' said one of the 'flower ladies' in the church. She's right of course.

Out on the north side is a fine table-tomb and against its west side leans a stone to Diana Maria Faith, Princess of Lowenstein Westhem, who died in 1967. What's more, against the south side is one for Prince Leopold Lowenstein (died 1974) and on the east side one to Constance Von Alversleren (died 1968).

The table tomb is for The Right Honourable Henry Baron Pirbright. The inscriptions tell you all about him. That on the north side seems to review his whole political career! The local connection is with Henley Park of which he was a tenant. That is a place steeped in history, with many royal and national connections, going right back to Saxon times but unfortunately it's not open to view.

What you will see here are woods and fields, still surviving between the developed areas of Ash and Guildford. The church is beside the A323, at the junction with Westwood Lane. Its only real point of interest is that it was the first church by Henry Woodyer. He did much work in Surrey, some of it his best and became a Victorian architect of note.